The Global Outlook for Government Debt over the Next 25 Years:
Implications for the Economy and Public Policy

The Global Outlook for Government Debt over the Next 25 Years:
Implications for the Economy and Public Policy

Joseph E. Gagnon
with Marc Hinterschweiger

PETERSON INSTITUTE FOR INTERNATIONAL ECONOMICS
Washington, DC
June 2011

Joseph E. Gagnon, senior fellow since September 2009, was visiting associate director, Division of Monetary Affairs (2008–09) at the US Federal Reserve Board. Previously he served at the US Federal Reserve Board as associate director, Division of International Finance (1999–2008), and senior economist (1987–90 and 1991–97). He has also served at the US Treasury Department (1994–95 and 1997–99) and has taught at the University of California's Haas School of Business (1990–91). He has published numerous articles in economics journals, including the *Journal of International Economics, Journal of Monetary Economics, Review of International Economics*, and *Journal of International Money and Finance*, and has contributed to several edited volumes. He received a BA from Harvard University in 1981 and a PhD in economics from Stanford University in 1987.

Marc Hinterschweiger has been a research analyst with the Peterson Institute since 2008. He is also a PhD candidate in economics at Ludwig-Maximilians University (LMU) in Munich, Germany. His research focuses on the transmission mechanism of monetary policy, asset prices, and financial crises. He previously worked at the Rhenish-Westfalian Institute for Economic Research (RWI) in Essen, Germany. He holds a BA in economics (2005) and a BA in international affairs (2006) from the University of St. Gallen, Switzerland. He earned a master's degree in public policy from Harvard University's Kennedy School of Government (2008), where he was a McCloy scholar specializing in international trade and finance. He has been a member of the German National Academic Foundation (Studienstiftung des deutschen Volkes) since 2002.

**PETER G. PETERSON INSTITUTE
FOR INTERNATIONAL ECONOMICS**
1750 Massachusetts Avenue, NW
Washington, DC 20036-1903
(202) 328-9000   FAX: (202) 659-3225
www.piie.com

C. Fred Bergsten, *Director*
Edward A. Tureen, *Director of Publications,
Marketing, and Web Development*

Printing by Versa Press, Inc.

Printed in the United States of America.

13   12   11   5   4   3   2   1

Library of Congress Cataloging-in-Publication Data
Gagnon, Joseph E.
  The global outlook for government debt over the next 25 years : implications for the economy and public policy / Joseph E. Gagnon, Marc Hinterschweiger.
    p. cm.
  Includes bibliographical references.
  ISBN 978-0-88132-621-5
  1. Debts, Public. 2. Economic policy. 3. Fiscal policy. I. Hinterschweiger, Marc. II. Title.
  HJ8015.G34 2011
  336.3'435--dc22

                                2011013376

Contents

Figures

Box

Preface

This Policy Analysis addresses a fundamentally new feature of the contemporary world economy: the simultaneous buildup of very large public deficits and debt positions in virtually all of the advanced high-income countries. The recent financial crisis sharply accelerated this fiscal deterioration but it was already well underway in some countries, including the United States, where demographic prospects had posed extremely worrisome trajectories for a number of years.

The study has three basic purposes. First, it projects the global fiscal outlook to 2035. Second, it asks whether the combination of deficits and debt in a large number of countries at the same time produces an impact on the world economy that is qualitatively different from the more traditional emergence of such problems in one or a few countries in any given period. Third, it analyzes the effects of the fiscal prospects on key economic variables including global interest rates and growth rates.

The analysis concludes that the current public debt profiles in most advanced economies will grow to dangerous and unsustainable levels over the next couple of decades unless major changes are made in projected spending and revenue levels. Critical questions raised include the likely nature and timing of future crises, and hence the policy strategies that countries should undertake to prevent such outcomes without jeopardizing recovery from the Great Recession. The authors conclude that the United States and Japan, in particular, need to start planning now for significant future budget cuts to minimize the risk of a crisis. Acting soon enables the adjustment to be phased in over an extended period, which cushions the inevitable adjustment costs, while avoiding the potentially enormous pressures that could be levied by markets if correction is delayed too long.

The Institute undertook this project at the request of the Peter G. Peterson Foundation, which is a completely separate entity. The Foundation focuses much of its attention on the fiscal prospects and problems of the United States, and it asked the Institute to imbed those national issues in the global context to assess how that broader perspective might affect the outlook and especially the need for early policy action by the United States. This project follows up an earlier study that we conducted at the request of the Foundation on *The Long-Term International Economic Position of the United States*, which I edited and we released as Special Report 20 in May 2009, that analyzed the impact of alternative US budget scenarios on the external deficits and international debt position of the country to 2030.

The Peter G. Peterson Institute for International Economics is a private, nonprofit institution for the study and discussion of international economic policy. Its purpose is to analyze important issues in that area and to develop and communicate practical new approaches for dealing with them. The Institute is completely nonpartisan.

The Institute is funded by a highly diversified group of philanthropic foundations, private corporations, and interested individuals. About 35 percent of the Institute's resources in our latest fiscal year was provided by contributors outside the United States. This study, as noted, was supported by the Peter G. Peterson Foundation.

The Institute's Board of Directors bears overall responsibilities for the Institute and gives general guidance and approval to its research program, including the identification of topics that are likely to become important over the medium run (one to three years) and that should be addressed by the Institute. The director, working closely with the staff and outside Advisory Committee, is responsible for the development of particular projects and makes the final decision to publish an individual study.

The Institute hopes that its studies and other activities will contribute to building a stronger foundation for international economic policy around the world. We invite readers of these publications to let us know how they think we can best accomplish this objective.

C. Fred Bergsten
Director
March 2011

Acknowledgments

The authors thank Anders Åslund, Fred Bergsten, Richard Berner, Bill Cline, Morris Goldstein, Doug Hamilton, Simon Johnson, Ed McKelvey, Michael Mussa, John Olcay, Pete Peterson, Carmen Reinhart, Arvind Subramanian, Steve Weisman, Susan Tanaka, Ted Truman, David Walker, and participants at a meeting sponsored by the Peterson Foundation on September 27, 2010 for helpful comments and discussions. The opinions expressed are those of the authors and not necessarily those of the Peterson Institute for International Economics or the Peter G. Peterson Foundation.

The Global Outlook for Government Debt over the Next 25 Years: Implications for the Economy and Public Policy

Overview

In their extraordinary coordinated response to the global financial crisis of 2008–09, advanced economies issued government debt at a record pace and magnitude for peacetime. This deficit spending and the aggressive intervention by central banks no doubt helped to prevent the global economy from sinking into another Great Depression. But it also prompted anxiety in some circles about the potentially adverse long-term consequences of such drastic actions. For now, in the major advanced economies, investors have bought up the new debt avidly, keeping the rates of interest on government bonds near 50-year lows. On the other hand, investors have been much less keen to buy the rising debts of some peripheral members of the euro area, driving interest rates in these countries well above those of France and Germany. The interest rate increases were most acute for Greece and Ireland, forcing the governments in Athens and Dublin to take emergency loans from the European Union and the International Monetary Fund (IMF). Investors continue to demand elevated yields on government bonds issued by Greece, Ireland, Portugal, and, to a lesser extent, Spain and Italy.

According to some analysts, officials, and bankers, the euro-area debt crisis is a harbinger of the dangers of indebtedness and deficit-spending for all countries. They note that over the long term, on top of the most recent government actions, nearly all countries face ageing populations and rising health care costs, which are certain to put further pressure on government budgets and on their ability to fund their spending. There is concern that these problems could lead to a rise in interest rates on sovereign debt and even a debt crisis—if not now, then eventually—although there is little agreement on what form such a crisis might take.

This book explores whether, and to what extent, interest rates could rise sharply in the major advanced economies, including the United States. What would trigger a fiscal crisis in the major advanced economies? What are the long-run implications of rising interest rates on public debt for economic growth rates? How quickly should governments tackle this problem and what are the costs of delay? Of particular interest is the global nature of the increased fiscal deficits. How unprecedented is the run-up of government debt relative to the size of the global economy? What are the limits to the global increase in public debt?

That government debt will grow to dangerous and unsustainable levels in most advanced and many emerging economies over the next 25 years—if there are no changes in current tax rates or government benefit programs in retirement and health care—is virtually beyond dispute. Whether interest rates might rise slowly or rapidly, whether some currencies might depreciate sharply, or whether some other form of crisis might occur is of course highly speculative. For the major economies and the world more broadly, in the absence of any large and unexpected negative shock to economic growth, the danger zone is likely to be relatively far into the future, about 10 to 25 years ahead. Over the next 5 to 10 years, debt ratios are not projected to reach dangerous levels in most economies, including in the United States.

If government debt is allowed to grow as projected, interest rates eventually will rise, crowding out productive investments and slowing down the rate of economic growth. High and rising levels of debt would make it difficult or impossible for governments to respond forcefully to any future economic downturn. Indeed, a serious economic downturn in the future could quickly push government debt levels more rapidly into the danger zone and greatly increase the chances of a crisis.

Although we have time to act, time is not on our side. In the near term, spending cuts and tax increases should not be implemented in the next two years in the United States, the euro area, and Japan, to allow the economic recovery to achieve more solid footing. In this regard, the recent tax cuts announced in the United States are appropriate because they delay the onset of fiscal tightening for another year. However, the lack of any concrete steps toward long-run fiscal consolidation in recent US legislation is regrettable, and it contributed, at least in part, to the modest rise of long-term interest rates in late December 2010. The bond rating agency, Moody's Investors Service (2011), recently warned that pressures from entitlement programs and deficit spending during the recession increase the likelihood of a negative outlook on the US credit rating being adopted over the next two years.

There are many reasons why policymakers should begin the process now of planning for an adjustment to a sustainable path for government debt. First, adopting a credible long-run plan now to reduce fiscal deficits in the future can reassure the markets, keep interest rates low, and instill greater confidence and certainty about future tax and spending policies, thereby encouraging businesses to commit their resources to job-creating investment projects. In addition, it is undeniable that fiscal retrenchment accomplished over an extended period of time is less painful than when it is carried out abruptly under the pressure of a crisis. Accordingly, we propose that budget cuts currently being planned should be implemented in 2013–15 and that additional budget cuts should begin in 2016, although there is some scope for additional cuts in Japan starting in 2014. In addition, reaching agreement soon on long-run changes to curb retirement and medical costs even partially could send a signal to markets that advanced governments are prepared to deal with a problem that threatens to grow more serious in the next two or three decades.

Introduction

The financial crisis of 2008 brought about the most rapid increase in global government debt since World War II (Abbas et al., 2010b, p. 1). The International Monetary Fund (IMF 2010b) projects that, between 2007 and 2011, net general government debt (as a percent of GDP) will rise from 51 percent to 70 percent in the euro area, from 42 percent to 73 percent in the United States, from 38 percent to 74 percent in the United Kingdom, and from 82 percent to 130 percent in Japan.

The deficit spending that created this debt explosion helped to prevent the global economy from sinking into another Great Depression. More specifically, the newly issued public debt supported aggregate demand while the private sector retreated, defaulting on mortgages and loans in some cases, and also deleveraging and restructuring its balance sheet quickly. Suddenly, public sector debt became more attractive to frightened investors, and interest rates on government debt fell to their lowest levels in decades. Long-term interest rates in the major advanced economies remain near multi-decade lows. Financial markets in these economies appear to be more concerned at present over the weak prospects for economic recovery than they are about rising public sector debt levels. As a result, governments in these economies continue to have scope to support economic activity through fiscal deficits in the near term.

The same is not true for several smaller euro-area countries, however. Starting last spring, financial market concerns about the ability of these governments to service their debts led to sharp increases in interest rates on government bonds. It seems likely that the Greek government would not have been able to sell bonds at any interest rate in the absence of intervention by its European partners and the IMF, which provided a large emergency loan. Even though Ireland's government did not need to borrow until mid-2011, it also turned to the European Union and the IMF for an emergency loan to help forestall a run on Irish banks, which are supported by government guarantees. Significantly, both of these emergency loans came in conjunction with severe austerity plans for the Greek and Irish governments. Markets are also worried about the ability of Portugal and Spain to service their public debts.

For the global economy more broadly, there are reasons to be worried about the build-up of government debt over the long run. Even after economies recover and temporary stimulus measures are withdrawn, many governments face significant budget deficits. All face trend increases in the costs of public pensions and health care as their populations age. There is a widespread debate about whether governments should continue stimulus programs or move toward fiscal consolidation out of concern that the experiences of Greece and Ireland could spread elsewhere. The G-20 group of major economic powers has held a series of summit conferences since the onset of the crisis in 2008, and yet these nations remain divided over this issue. In Toronto, they sought to resolve their differences by agreeing to a timetable for fiscal adjustment after the hoped-for end of the current crisis. Their statement at the end of that meeting alluded to their differences even while setting out a goal of reducing deficits within three years:

> Sound fiscal finances are essential to sustain recovery, provide flexibility to respond to new shocks, ensure the capacity to meet the challenges of ageing populations, and avoid leaving future generations with a legacy of deficits and debt. The path of adjustment must be carefully calibrated to sustain the recovery in private demand. There is a risk that synchronized fiscal adjustment across several major economies could adversely impact the recovery. There is also a risk that the failure to implement consolidation where necessary would undermine confidence and hamper growth. Reflecting this balance, advanced economies have committed to fiscal plans that will at least halve deficits by 2013 and stabilize or reduce government debt-to-GDP ratios by 2016. (*The G20 Toronto Summit Declaration*, 2010, paragraph 10)

In Seoul, Leaders reaffirmed their Toronto commitment on fiscal policies without further elaboration.

This book explores the long-run fiscal outlook for key economies and the world overall. We project scenarios for future economic growth, interest rates, and government debt under current fiscal plans, including current benefit formulas for public pensions and public health care. The purpose is not to forecast the most likely outcomes. Rather it is to highlight the fact that current policies are unsustainable under a range of plausible circumstances, and to underscore the importance of actions to achieve the G-20 goals on reducing deficits.

Projected Paths of Government Debt

General Government Primary Balances

The starting point for this analysis is a set of projections by the IMF for general government primary balances in 2015.[1] These projections are based on policies adopted as of year-end 2010, and they incorporate the effects of announced

---

1. The primary balance is the difference between non-interest government revenues and spending on government programs. The primary balance excludes net interest payments. Because primary balances are negative in most economies, the discussion below refers to deficits rather than balances in order to avoid a plethora of minus signs. Data are from IMF (2010c) with updates for 2010–12 from IMF (2011).

government plans for specific spending cuts and revenue increases, even if these plans have not been formally enacted. The projections also assume that economic recovery will boost government revenues. For 2015, we use the cyclically adjusted primary balance.[2] The cyclically adjusted balance is a better starting point for extrapolating debt because GDP should be close to potential on average over the long run. The projections imply substantial declines in primary deficits over the next five years. As with any forecast, there is considerable uncertainty surrounding these projections, and they may well prove too optimistic. Nevertheless, they are a reasonable place to start the analysis. The top row of table 1 displays the projected primary deficits for 2015.[3]

We assume that the primary deficit would remain constant as a percent of GDP in the years beyond 2015 as long as GDP remains close to trend and there are no special factors, which we will discuss shortly. In other words, we assume that revenues and expenditures grow in proportion to GDP and therefore result in primary deficits that also remain in the same proportion to GDP. One special factor that tends to increase the primary deficit over time is the effect of population ageing and rising health-care costs on public pensions and public health care spending.[4] The second and third rows of table 1 display estimates from the Organization of Economic Cooperation and Development (OECD) of the annual average increases in these costs over the period 2010 through 2025 under the assumption that current benefits formulas and contribution rates remain unchanged.[5] Note that most of the increased spending is attributed to health care and not public pensions. We assume that these costs continue to rise at the same rates in the years after 2025. These rising costs of social benefits cause expected primary deficits to increase in all economies after 2015.

Another special factor affecting primary deficits is the projected slowing of GDP growth associated with rising public debts, as discussed below. We assume that any reduction of GDP below its previous trend increases the primary deficit by an amount proportional to the share of government revenues in GDP. The fourth row of table 1 shows the implied levels of primary deficits in 2035 under our baseline scenario after taking into consideration the above special factors.

---

2. Cyclical adjustment removes the effect of any shortfall or excess of actual GDP relative to potential GDP on revenues and spending programs that respond directly to GDP. In other words, it is an estimate of what the balance would be if GDP were at potential.

3. The advanced-economy aggregate is based on the IMF definition of advanced economies. It includes the United States, the euro area, and Japan, as well as other economies. The emerging-economy aggregate includes 27 important developing economies.

4. In the United States, "public pensions" refers to the Social Security old age and disability insurance programs and "public health care" refers to Medicare and Medicaid.

5. See OECD (2010b). The recent increase in the French retirement age is not factored into these estimates.

Table 1   Fiscal and economic assumptions

	United States	Euro area	Japan	Advanced economies	Emerging economies
Deficit components (percent of GDP)					
Baseline primary deficit (level in 2015)	2.0	−0.3	5.0	1.1	−0.6
Public pensions (annual increase)	.05	.05	.01	.06	.06
Public health care (annual increase)	.10	.15	.18	.12	.06
Baseline primary deficit (level in 2035)	7.7	5.6	11.4	6.7	2.3
Health care alternatives					
Optimistic (annual increase)	.04	.05	.06	.05	.02
Pessimistic (annual increase)	.25	.27	.26	.25	.10
2016–35 real GDP growth rate (percent)					
OECD 2016–25	2.4	1.6	1.1	2.2	5.0
Baseline	1.9	1.4	0.6	1.8	5.0
Optimistic	2.6	2.1	1.2	2.5	5.0
Pessimistic	1.0	1.1	−0.3	1.1	4.6
2016–35 nominal GDP growth rate in US dollars (percent)					
Baseline	3.9	3.4	2.6	3.9	8.0
Optimistic	4.6	4.1	3.2	4.6	8.0
Pessimistic	3.0	3.1	1.7	3.2	7.6

OECD = Organization for Economic Cooperation and Development

Notes: OECD health care projections include publicly funded long-term care. OECD projections are based on the period 2010–25 and are assumed to grow at the same rate in 2026–35. IMF projections are based on the period 2010–30 and are assumed to grow at the same rate in 2031–35. Advanced and emerging economies are based on IMF definitions. The advanced-economy aggregate includes the United States, the euro area, Japan, and other countries included in the IMF definition of advanced economies. The pension reforms recently passed by the French parliament are not factored into these estimates.

Sources: The baseline primary deficits in 2015 are cyclically adjusted primary deficits from IMF (2010c). Pension and health care projections are from OECD (2010b, Table 4.5). Health care alternatives are from IMF (2010a). Baseline growth rates are described in the text and are based on OECD (2010b, Table 4.2), and, for emerging economies, OECD (2010a, Table 4.2). Emerging economy growth rates are an unweighted average of rates for Brazil, China, India, Indonesia, Mexico, and Russia. Emerging-economy currencies are assumed to appreciate against advanced-economy currencies at an annual rate of 1 percent in real terms. Optimistic and pessimistic growth rates are described in the text.

Size of Economies (GDP)

In order to construct global debt measures, we project each economy's GDP in terms of US dollars. From 2005 through 2015, we use IMF data and projections. For 2016–25, OECD (2010b) projects GDP growth rates and inflation rates under the assumption that net government debt ratios gradually stabilize by 2025. We use the OECD growth and inflation projections for our baseline estimates for 2016–20. Beginning in 2021, as net debt in our baseline scenario rises above that in the OECD projection, we reduce the GDP growth rates from those in the OECD projection in proportion to the growth in the ratio of net general government debt to GDP, assuming that each percentage point increase in the net debt ratio permanently reduces GDP by 0.03 percent.[6] This effect occurs either because of rising interest rates or because of heightened uncertainty on the part of businesses and investors about future policies. We do not factor in any effect of the debt ratio on inflation, which is near 2 percent in all regions. We assume constant real exchange rates among the advanced economies and we assume that emerging economies experience an annual real appreciation against the advanced economies of 1 percent.[7]

The bottom half of table 1 displays the OECD projected real growth rates that are the basis of our projections. For each of the advanced regions, the baseline GDP growth rate is lower than the OECD projection on average, reflecting the negative effect of rising debt on GDP. This effect does not begin to affect emerging economies until the very end of the projection period. As described below, we also consider scenarios with more optimistic and more pessimistic growth rates, which are shown at the bottom of table 1.

Interest Rates

Interest rates have an important effect on any projection of government debt. For a given path of primary deficits, the future debt level will be higher if the government has to pay higher interest on its debt. Averaged over long periods of time, effective government interest rates in most economies have been close to average nominal GDP growth rates.[8] We use the IMF projections of effective government interest rates through 2014, which are generally lower than

---

6. An effect of this size is incorporated in the OECD's macroeconomic model.

7. These paths for real exchange rates are not consistent with real interest rate parity across countries, but they are consistent with a constant relative purchasing power parity after allowing for a modest effect of faster productivity growth in developing economies relative to advanced economies. There is much more empirical support for long-run purchasing power parity than long-run real interest rate parity.

8. The effective interest rate equals government net interest payments divided by net government debt. It is essentially a weighted average of the interest rates of outstanding bonds. Appendix 1 of IMF (2010c) shows that long-term bond yields in advanced economies generally exceeded growth rates in 1981–2000 and were close to growth rates in 2001–08. However, the 1981–2000 period was characterized by generalized disinflation that pushed nominal growth rates below nominal bond yields. The opposite phenomenon occurred in the 1960s and 1970s, and growth rates generally were above bond yields in 1960–80. Moreover, the effective interest rate on government debt tends to be lower than the long-term bond yield because a significant fraction of debt is issued at short maturities. In emerging economies, bond yields tend to be lower than nominal growth rates.

projected nominal GDP growth rates in 2011–14. In 2015 we assume that the effective interest rate equals the trend growth rate of nominal GDP.

A major concern about rising government debt is its potential to crowd out productive investment through higher interest rates, especially as debt ratios rise above historical ranges.[9] As discussed in box 1, "Statistical Estimates of the Effect of Government Debt on Interest Rates," recent studies have found surprising agreement as to the size of the effect of rising debt ratios on interest rates. Beginning in 2016, we assume that the effective interest rate equals the growth rate of nominal GDP plus an additional amount related to the growth of a country's ratio of net government debt to GDP. Based on a mid-range estimate from existing studies, the interest rate rises above the nominal growth rate by 3.5 basis points for each percentage point increase in the ratio of net debt to GDP above its 2014 level.[10] This feedback from debt to interest rates exacerbates the cost of serving that debt over time, which in turn makes the reduction of fiscal deficits more difficult.

Baseline Debt Projections Differ for Advanced and Emerging Economies

Table 2 and figures 1 to 6 display projections for general government net debt as a percent of GDP through 2035, showing a significant difference in the projected experience of advanced versus emerging economies. General government includes all levels of government (central, regional, and local) as well as government-run benefits programs. It does not include publicly owned corporations that operate on a market basis without routine subsidies. Net debt is defined as all financial liabilities minus all financial assets of the government sector. Net debt is the appropriate concept for evaluating long-run solvency.[11]

Under the baseline scenario, general government net debt in the United States is projected to rise from 65 percent of GDP in 2010 to 99 percent of GDP in 2020 and 213 percent of GDP in 2035. The increase is more muted in the euro area, rising to only 133 percent of GDP by 2035. In Japan, however, the increase is dramatic. Japanese net debt is estimated to have been 121 percent of

---

9. Higher interest rates may also encourage additional saving, which reduces the crowding-out of productive investment. However, most economists believe the effects of interest rates on investment are greater than the effects on saving.

10. In light of very low interest rates in Japan despite record debt levels, we reduce this effect by 50 percent for Japan. OECD (2010b, Chapter 4) assumes a slightly larger effect (4 basis points versus 3.5) except for Japan, where the effect is 1 basis point.

11. For many countries, gross debt and net debt are nearly equal. In the United States, gross debt exceeds net debt by a significant amount because the Social Security system holds Treasury bonds. Most other countries have a pay-as-you-go public pension system which holds few financial assets. One of the main purposes of extrapolating deficits and debt out for 25 years is to calculate the extent to which public pension systems are underfunded. Thus, to use gross debt for the United States would double-count the cost of future Social Security deficits.

Box 1 Statistical estimates of the effect of government debt on interest rates

The effect of government debt on interest rates has been an active field of research. Many papers analyze the effect of both budget deficits and debt, but, from a theoretical point of view, the long-run effect on interest rates should be a consequence of the latter. Thus, we focus on the estimated effects of government debt. These papers all examine the effects on real interest rates, either by using measures of the real interest rate as regressands or by including measures of inflation expectations as regressors.

Engen and Hubbard (2005) find that an increase in US federal debt by 1 percentage point (pp) leads to an increase in the long-term real interest rate by roughly 3 to 5 basis points (bps), depending on the time period. Laubach's (2009) estimates are in the same range. Gale and Orszag (2004) find a slightly higher range of 3 to 6 bps. All of these studies use forward long-term interest rates and projected future values of the fiscal variables. Because the business cycle has opposite effects on interest rates and the fiscal position, using current values of these variables would introduce a negative correlation between these variables that biases downward estimates of the long-run relationship.

Focusing on a panel of OECD countries, Chinn and Frankel (2007) obtain a wide range of estimates, both negative and positive, perhaps because of their very short sample. We do not include their results in the table below. Kinoshita (2006) obtains results very similar to those described for the United States above. Gruber and Kamin (2010) obtain results at the low end of those described above. Baldacci and Kumar (2010) use panel regressions including both advanced and major developing economies. They, too, find an effect of about 3 to 5 bps.

(continued on next page)

GDP in 2010, and it is projected to rise to 183 percent of GDP in 2020 and 386 percent in 2035. For the advanced economies in aggregate, net debt is projected to rise from 67 percent of GDP in 2010 to 90 percent of GDP in 2020 and 178 percent in 2035. Net debt is much lower in the emerging economies—only 27 percent of GDP in 2010. It is projected to edge down to 24 percent of GDP in 2020 and then rise to only 40 percent in 2035. For the world, net debt is estimated to have been 54 percent of GDP in 2010, rising to 61 percent of GDP in 2020 and 98 percent of GDP in 2035.[12]

---

12. Mrsnik et al. (2010) project a median general government net debt of around 140 percent of GDP in 2035 for a sample of 32 advanced and 17 emerging markets on current policies. Although this projection is somewhat higher than our projection for average world debt, the Mrsnik sample

Box 1   Statistical estimates of the effect of government debt on interest rates *(continued)*

Conway and Orr (2002) and Ardagna, Caselli, and Lane (2004) find that the relationship between long-term interest rates and public debt is non-linear. They estimate that when government debt is 100 percent of GDP, a 1 pp increase in debt raises long-term interest rates about 1 bp, a value that is lower than the other estimates. However, Ardagna, Caselli, and Lane find that this effect increases to 3.5 bps when debt is 140 percent of GDP.

Study	Effect of 1 pp debt increase on real long-term interest rate	Countries	Time period
Conway & Orr (2002)	1 bp (for debt at 100 percent of GDP but rising for higher debt levels)	OECD countries	1986–2002
Ardagna, Caselli, & Lane (2004)			1960–2002
Gale & Orzag (2004)	3-6 bps	US	1976–2004
Engen & Hubbard (2005)	3-5 bps	US	1953/76– 2003
Kinoshita (2006)	2-5 bps	OECD countries	1971–2004
Laubach (2009)	3-5 bps	US	1976–2005
Baldacci & Kumar (2010)	3-5 bps	31 countries	1980–2008
Gruber & Kamin (2010)	2 bps	G-7 countries	1988–2007

For the United States, the baseline projection is moderately higher than that implied by the Congressional Budget Office's "Alternative" (CBO-A) projection of federal debt held by the public.[13] The main reason for the discrepancy is that our baseline allows for a negative effect on future GDP growth from rising government debt, whereas the CBO projection does not factor in any negative effect of debt on GDP.[14] Without the negative feedback of debt

---

is composed primarily of advanced economies, for which we project an even higher average debt ratio.

13. Until the financial crisis of 2008, debt held by the public was essentially equal to net federal debt. CBO (2011) estimates that, at the end of 2010, the value of federal claims on the financial sector was 7 percent of GDP. The IMF net debt estimates for the United States do not appear to subtract these holdings.

14. Our baseline projection also takes into account the relatively small and stable amount of state and local net debt that is included in the general government baseline—about 5 percent of GDP as of this year. Due to balanced budget provisions in most state constitutions, state and local debts are not expected to expand at the same rate as federal debt. Another difference is that our projec-

Table 2 General government net debt projections (percent of GDP)

	2005	2010	2015	2020	2035
United States					
Optimistic growth	43	65	86	97	155
Baseline	43	65	86	99	213
Pessimistic growth	43	65	86	99	302
Pessimistic health cost	43	65	86	103	331
High interest rates	43	65	86	100	270
CBO-A (federal debt held by the public)	37	62	73	87	185
Euro area					
Optimistic growth	55	67	73	74	72
Baseline	55	67	73	76	133
Pessimistic growth	55	67	73	76	155
Pessimistic health cost	55	67	73	80	224
High interest rates	55	67	73	76	144
Japan					
Optimistic growth	85	121	153	181	335
Baseline	85	121	153	183	386
Pessimistic growth	85	121	153	183	504
Pessimistic health cost	85	121	153	185	435
High interest rates	85	121	153	185	482
Advanced economies					
Optimistic growth	48	67	81	88	122
Baseline	48	67	81	90	178
Pessimistic growth	48	67	81	90	234
Pessimistic health cost	48	67	81	94	276
High interest rates	48	67	81	91	210
Emerging economies					
Optimistic growth	34	27	26	23	35
Baseline	34	27	26	24	40
Pessimistic growth	34	27	26	25	59
Pessimistic health cost	34	27	26	24	54
High interest rates	34	27	26	24	40
World					
Optimistic growth	45	54	59	60	74
Baseline	45	54	59	61	98
Pessimistic growth	45	54	59	62	130
Pessimistic health cost	45	54	59	64	144
High interest rates	45	54	59	61	110

Note: CBO-A is based on CBO (2010a). CBO (2011) has higher estimates for 2015 and 2020 (around 80 and 95 percent, respectively) but does not extend to 2035.

Source: Author calculations and IMF fiscal data and projections for 2005–14.

Figure 1   General government net debt projections—United States

percent of GDP

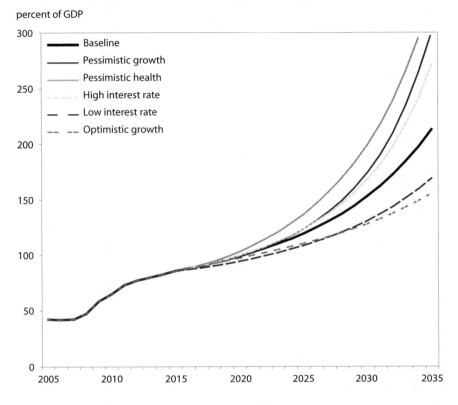

Source: Author calculations and IMF fiscal data and projections for 2005–14.

on growth, our baseline would imply a ratio of net debt to GDP in 2035 of 194 percent (versus 213 percent with the negative feedback). For US federal debt, it is widely agreed that the CBO-A projection is more realistic than the CBO baseline projection, because it embodies relatively realistic assumptions about future actions to address the issue.[15]

---

15. See CBO (2010a). The CBO baseline debt projection assumes that all the Bush tax cuts are allowed to expire, that coverage of the alternative minimum tax is expanded considerably, that Medicare payments to doctors will not be increased, and that other types of spending will decline as a share of GDP. The CBO-A debt projection assumes that the Bush tax cuts will be extended for most households, that the alternative minimum tax will not be allowed to expand, that Medicare payments will be increased, and that other spending will grow in line with GDP. CBO (2011) presents a revised version of the alternative projection that incorporates the effects of recent legislation. This projection does not extend beyond 2021, but it does show federal debt held by the public of around 80 percent of GDP in 2015 and 95 percent of GDP in 2020.

Figure 2   General government net debt projections—Japan

percent of GDP

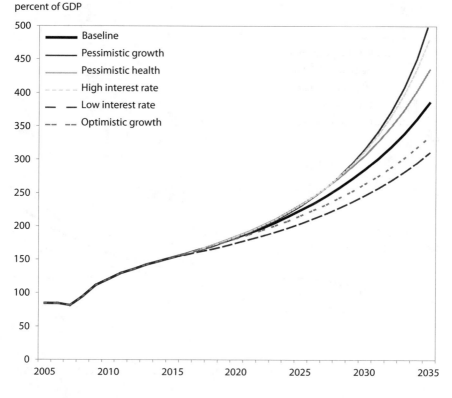

Source: Author calculations and IMF fiscal data and projections for 2005–14.

The large increases in net debt in our baseline scenario should not be viewed as a forecast of likely outcomes. Rather they should be understood to indicate the magnitude of the looming fiscal challenges. For the United States and Japan, the challenges in the baseline scenario are so great that a crisis is likely to happen before 2035 if policies are not corrected. We return to the issues of fiscal crises and policy options later.

Two factors explain why the global increase in debt as a share of global GDP is considerably less than the increase in advanced economies only. First, debt ratios in the emerging economies are projected to grow much more slowly than in the advanced economies, and they are not projected to grow at all over the next 10 years. Second, GDP in the emerging economies is growing more rapidly than in the advanced economies. In what will likely be a transforming shift in the wealth and prosperity of different parts of the globe over the next generation or two, the emerging economies' share of global GDP is projected to rise from 34 percent in 2010 to 58 percent in 2035. The implications for the

Figure 3 General government net debt projections—Euro area

percent of GDP

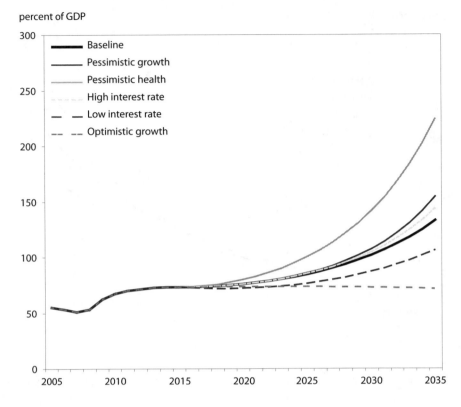

Source: Author calculations and IMF fiscal data and projections for 2005–14.

ability of the advanced economies to market their growing debt are impossible to predict. To some extent, the emerging economies have been and may continue to be a natural buyer of advanced-economy government debt. But, as discussed later, under some scenarios the projected increases in the net debt ratio for the emerging economies by 2035 are large relative to their historical experience and possibly unsustainable. Moreover, the increasing depth and efficiency of emerging financial markets may tempt governments in these economies to run larger fiscal deficits than projected. Both developments would tend to reduce the ability of emerging markets to absorb advanced-economy government debt.

The Optimistic and Pessimistic Health Care Cost Scenarios

By far the most important contributor to concerns about mounting government debts and deficits is the exploding cost of health care over the next several decades. As many studies have demonstrated, these costs result from

Figure 4   General government net debt projections—Advanced economies

percent of GDP

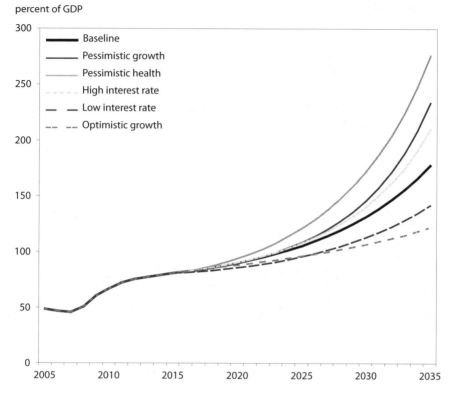

Source: Author calculations and IMF fiscal data and projections for 2005–14.

three factors: (1) an ageing population, (2) the increasing cost of medical technologies and technological breakthroughs that become a basic part of what patients expect, and (3) the poorly organized and inefficient incentives that drive up costs in the American health care system, in particular. But there is considerable uncertainty surrounding the future path of public health care expenses, even with the benefit formulas and contribution rates held constant. A recent study by the IMF (2010a) presents both optimistic and pessimistic projections of health care costs, which are shown in the middle rows of table 1.[16] By the year 2035, the annual increase in health care costs under the pessimistic assumptions leads to a net increase in health costs that exceeds those

---

16. IMF (2010d) updated these estimates, mainly lowering the pessimistic projections, especially in Europe. We chose not to use the updated estimates because they seemed too low compared to those of the OECD.

Figure 5   General government net debt projections—Emerging economies

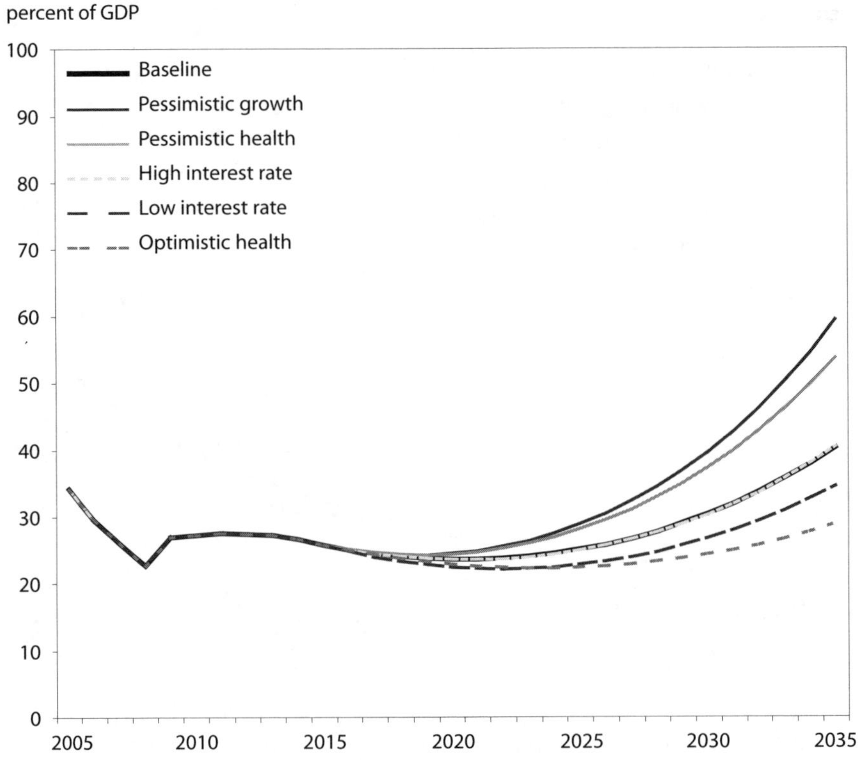

percent of GDP

Source: Author calculations and IMF fiscal data and projections for 2005–14.

under the optimistic assumptions by about 4 percent of GDP in each of the advanced economies and 1½ percent of GDP in the emerging economies. The major sources of this uncertainty are health care technology and the scope for improvements in the efficiency of health care delivery.

For each of the advanced economies, the projected future debt ratios under the optimistic health care scenario are only modestly lower than those of the baseline scenario. To save space, they are not displayed in table 2 or figures 1–4 and 6. For the emerging markets, the optimistic health care scenario is shown in figure 5, and it has the lowest path of debt among the scenarios. The future debt ratios under the pessimistic health care scenario are displayed in table 2 and figures 1–6. These are significantly higher than those under the baseline scenario for all regions.

Figure 6   General government net debt projections—World

percent of GDP

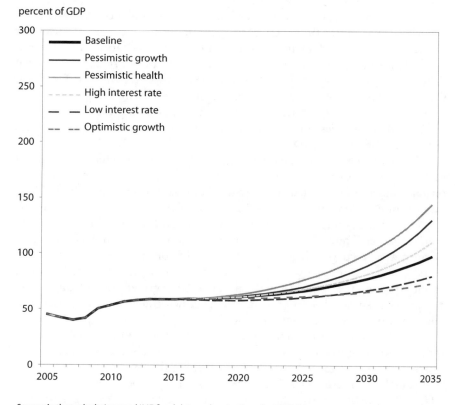

Source: Author calculations and IMF fiscal data and projections for 2005–14.

Two Interest Rate Scenarios

Because there is considerable uncertainty about the future path of interest rates, this book projects the ability of governments to cope with higher deficits and debts under two alternative interest rate scenarios, one optimistic and the other more dire.

The "low interest rates" scenario is based on the implied prediction of low future interest rates built into current long-term bond yields. For example, the 10-year interest rate in the United States is around 3½ percent and the 30-year rate is around 4½ percent. These rates appear to indicate that markets expect short-term interest rates to remain low for decades. It is unlikely, however, that interest rates would remain low over the next 20 to 30 years if government debt were to rise as projected in the baseline scenario. To the extent that rates are low, it is probably because financial market participants expect that governments will take steps, however unknown or undefined, to prevent such alarming increases in debt over the long run.

Despite the hope of many that deficits will come under control over time, we believe that most US market participants do not expect faster fiscal cuts in the next few years than are built into our baseline scenario.[17] Thus, it may be reasonable to assume that long-term interest rates will remain low even if debt ratios rise as projected in the baseline scenario over the next few years. Current 5-year forward interest rates, at 2-year and 5-year maturities, are a good measure of market expectations of government borrowing costs in 2015. For the United States, these rates are around 4 to 5 percent, close to the projected growth rate of nominal GDP.

Effective interest rates tend to adjust slowly to any change in market interest rates. This is because effective interest rates include the rates paid on long term bonds issued many years previous. For example, the effective interest rates estimated by the IMF for each of these economies in 2010 are higher than the average yields on newly issued government debt. Accordingly, even if market interest rates were to rise according to the implied prediction of current yield curves, the effective rates might continue to decline for a few years. The low interest rates scenario thus assumes that effective rates stay about 1 percentage point below the nominal GDP growth rate through 2015 and then rise smoothly in proportion to the growing debt ratio using the same relationship as in the baseline scenario.

To save space the low interest rate scenario is not included in table 2 but it is displayed in figures 1–6. In all regions, the future debt ratios under the low interest rates scenario are lower than those under the baseline scenario.

The "high interest rates" scenario uses a larger coefficient (5.5) for the effect of the debt ratio on the interest rate (compared to 3.5 in the baseline scenario).[18] This estimate is near the high end of the range discussed in box 1. With a larger effect of debt on interest rates, the dynamics of fiscal deficits multiply rapidly and debt ratios rise well above baseline, except in the emerging markets, where debts are on a downward trajectory for the next 10 to 15 years.

The Optimistic Growth Scenario

The baseline growth projections for the advanced economies are somewhat lower than their average growth rates before the global financial crisis, and there is little rebound from the recession of 2009. As shown in the bottom of table 1, the "optimistic growth" scenario assumes higher growth than the

---

17. See, for example, Lupton and Hensley (2010, p. 13), who forecast changes in primary balances between 2010 and 2013 for the euro area, Japan, and the United States that are close to those in our baseline scenario.

18. As in the other scenarios, the interest rate effect in Japan is assumed to be only half as large as in the other economies.

baseline GDP growth projections for advanced economies.[19] One factor that would make the optimistic growth scenario plausible is the potential for a global rebalancing of demand toward the advanced economies. Although China and some other emerging economies have been slow to move in this direction, they are likely to come under increasing pressure to do so in the future. In such a rebalancing, emerging economies with large current account surpluses would allow their exchange rates to appreciate, reducing the rate at which they accumulate foreign exchange reserves and directing more of their savings to domestic projects. As a result, interest rates in this scenario decline 1 percentage point in the emerging economies and they rise by an amount equal to the increase in GDP growth rates in the advanced economies.

An increase in GDP, on the other hand, lowers primary deficits in advanced economies by an amount proportional to the share of general government gross revenues in GDP as projected by the IMF for 2015.[20] Table 2 and figures 1–4 and 6 show that relatively moderate but persistent increases in economic growth do significantly reduce projected debt ratios in the advanced economies and the world.[21] Sustained growth is thus, as always, an excellent remedy for deficits, however unsustainable they may be. But the higher growth rates projected in this scenario are not sufficient to prevent debt ratios from rising in the major economic regions—except for the euro area.

The Pessimistic Growth Scenario

The "pessimistic growth" scenario results from the fulfillment of fears that rising debts will choke off investment and threaten a potential crisis. In this sense, the scenario may be viewed as a crisis scenario, though the nature of an actual crisis—not to mention its effects—is extremely hard to predict. The pessimistic growth scenario deepens the negative drag on GDP that would result from rising debt ratios, reflecting the effects of "crowding out" of productive investment when governments run large deficits after economic activity has fully recovered from recession. Beginning in 2016, the levels of real and nominal GDP are reduced by 0.06 percent for each percent increase in the ratio of net government debt to GDP, double the effect in the baseline scenario. In addition, the effect of debt on interest rates is assumed to be the same as that assumed in the "high interest rates" scenario. These changes tend to increase GDP growth initially in emerging economies because their debt ratio is falling, so in this scenario we exogenously reduce GDP growth in the

---

19. Trend GDP growth in each advanced region is 0.5 percentage points higher than in the baseline after 2015. A small additional positive effect on growth occurs because of the reduced accumulation of public debt.

20. For example, when the revenue share is 50 percent, a one percent increase in GDP lowers the primary deficit 0.5 percentage points. See IMF (2010c).

21. The optimistic growth scenario is not included in figure 5 because it is identical to the low interest rate scenario for the emerging economies.

emerging economies by 0.5 percent per year. As shown in the bottom rows of table 1, this scenario implies a large reduction in the US growth rate and a negative average growth rate of Japanese real GDP. The pessimistic growth scenario may exaggerate the negative effect of government debt on GDP, but it does help to flesh out the range of possible outcomes.[22] The feedback from higher debt to both higher interest rates and lower GDP creates much larger increases in debt ratios over time in all economies.

Little Comfort from Net Debt Projections

None of the optimistic scenarios discussed above leads to a decline in net debt ratios for any economy, with the sole exception of the euro area under optimistic growth assumptions. Under more pessimistic assumptions about future economic growth, health care costs, or interest rates, the implied increases in net debt ratios by 2035 in all of the advanced economies are enormous. For all of the advanced regions, the large increases in debt under some of the pessimistic scenarios almost certainly are not feasible, and even the baseline path for debt is probably not feasible. These scenarios likely would lead to a fiscal crisis in which governments would be forced to choose some combination of higher taxes, reduced spending, default on debt, or monetization of debt before 2035. The limits of debt are the topic of the next section.

The Burden of Debt and Fiscal Limits

How much debt is "sustainable"? Ultimately, the level of sustainable debt depends not on some abstract formula, but on the willingness of society and government to pay the interest on the debt and to accept the reduction in GDP caused by the higher interest rates and higher tax rates associated with such a burden. There is no automatic way to calculate that effect but some obvious economic and financial norms do apply. The following analysis seeks to apply the lessons of history for understanding likely future developments. We note that our analysis does not make any strong assumptions about rationality or

---

22. Reinhart and Rogoff (2010) suggest that the effect of debt on GDP growth may be highly nonlinear, with relatively little effect when debt is less than 90 percent of GDP and a large effect when debt is greater than 90 percent of GDP. They do not estimate a specific functional relationship between debt and growth. Caner et al. (2010) and Checherita and Rother (2010) find significant nonlinear relationships between government debt and GDP growth for developing economies and euro-area economies, respectively, with inflection points around 70 to 100 percent of GDP. Kumar and Woo (2010) also find a negative effect of debt on GDP for a broad panel of advanced and developing economies. Irons and Bivens (2010) point out that the Reinhart-Rogoff result is heavily influenced by the experiences of developing economies with poor institutions and by major wars in advanced economies. They also suggest that the causality seems to run from low growth to high debt rather than the reverse. We note that the results of Caner et al., Checherita and Rother, and Kumar and Woo are obtained in samples dominated by government borrowing in currencies not under the control of the sovereign, for which interest rate effects and debt intolerance appear to be greater.

foresight of either the public or the private sector. However, there is no guarantee that markets or governments will behave the same in the future as they did in the past.

Effect of Debt on Interest Rates and Interest Payments

Table 3 and figures 7–11 display effective interest rates on government debt, both past and projected. Since 2006, interest rates have fallen in the United States and the euro area, in part because of the economic downturn, which led investors to buy government securities in dollars and euros as a safe haven, and in part because of the trend increase in reserve accumulation by many governments in developing economies. At the same time, rates have risen in Japan because of the end of the quantitative easing policy. In the baseline scenario, interest rates are projected to equal the trend growth rate of nominal GDP in all economies in 2015, roughly consistent with historical average behavior and the assumption that output will be near its long-run potential. This projection implicitly assumes that developing economies will slow their rapid purchases of bonds in the advanced economies.

What is significant is that beyond 2015, interest rates gradually rise in line with net debt ratios. The cumulative increase is most notable in the United States and Japan, where rates are at very low levels at present, but it is also significant in Europe. The projected levels of interest rates in 2035 may seem rather modest given the large increases in government debt in some regions. Three factors explain this muted rise in interest rates.

First, and perhaps most important, our estimates of the effect of government debt on interest rates essentially assume that there is no risk of default. This assumption is appropriate for governments that borrow in currencies they control because they can print money to pay their debts in extremity. The United States, the euro area as a whole, Japan, most other advanced economies, and some emerging economies borrow in currencies they control. But individual euro-area countries and many emerging economies borrow in currencies they do not control; in such cases, default becomes a serious risk when debt levels rise. A number of studies have found large effects of debt on interest rates for governments that borrow in currencies they do not control.[23]

Second, all of our scenarios assume constant low inflation and stable inflation expectations. There is no way of predicting how future fiscal developments would affect inflation and prices, but the behavior of central banks over the past 20 years suggests that there is a reasonable chance that inflation may

---

23. See, for example, Baldacci et al. (2008) and Bayoumi et al. (1995). Prior to 2008, bond yields in the euro area were not sensitive to debt ratios, probably reflecting market expectations that fiscal transfers would prevent any defaults. Despite the partial confirmation of these beliefs with the loan packages for Greece and Ireland, markets appear to have substantially revised upward their views concerning the possibility of future defaults or restructurings. See Caceres et al. (2010a), Haugh et al. (2009), Schuknecht et al. (2009), and Sgherri and Zoli (2009).

Table 3   Effective interest rate on government debt (percent)

	2006	2010	2015	2020	2035
United States					
Optimistic growth	4.8	2.8	4.4	5.3	6.4
Baseline	4.8	2.8	4.4	4.9	6.9
Pessimistic growth	4.8	2.8	4.4	4.7	9.7
Pessimistic health cost	4.8	2.8	4.4	5.0	8.9
High interest rates	4.8	2.8	4.4	5.2	10.6
Euro area					
Optimistic growth	4.8	4.0	3.6	4.1	4.1
Baseline	4.8	4.0	3.6	3.7	4.7
Pessimistic growth	4.8	4.0	3.6	3.7	5.6
Pessimistic health cost	4.8	4.0	3.6	3.8	6.3
High interest rates	4.8	4.0	3.6	3.7	5.9
Japan					
Optimistic growth	0.6	1.3	3.1	4.1	5.4
Baseline	0.6	1.3	3.1	3.6	5.4
Pessimistic growth	0.6	1.3	3.1	3.4	7.5
Pessimistic health cost	0.6	1.3	3.1	3.6	5.8
High interest rates	0.6	1.3	3.1	3.9	8.7
Advanced economies					
Optimistic growth	3.7	2.9	4.3	5.1	5.7
Baseline	3.7	2.9	4.3	4.6	6.1
Pessimistic growth	3.7	2.9	4.3	4.5	8.1
Pessimistic health cost	3.7	2.9	4.3	4.7	7.8
High interest rates	3.7	2.9	4.3	4.8	8.6
Emerging economies					
Optimistic growth	7.3	9.0	8.0	6.9	7.1
Baseline	7.3	9.0	8.0	7.9	8.2
Pessimistic growth	7.3	9.0	8.0	7.6	8.7
Pessimistic health cost	7.3	9.0	8.0	7.9	8.4
High interest rates	7.3	9.0	8.0	7.8	8.4

Source: Author calculations and IMF fiscal data and projections for 2005–14.

remain low even with large increases in debt. At some point, however, increases in the cost of servicing debt are bound to force governments to resort to inflationary money creation. If inflation were to increase significantly, interest rates would surely be even higher than projected here. But the real rate of interest

Figure 7 Effective interest rate on general government debt—United States

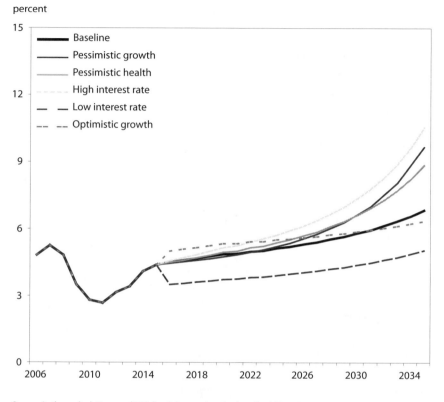

percent

Source: Author calculations and IMF fiscal data and projections for 2005–14.

(i.e., the nominal interest rate minus the expected inflation rate) might move by an amount consistent with the empirical results in table 3. Higher real rates of interest are the primary channel through which government budget deficits crowd out productive investment and ultimately reduce the growth rate of the economy.

The third, and probably least important, factor is that in our scenarios the increase in government debt restrains the growth of GDP, which holds down interest rates. This factor becomes significant only in the final few years of the more extreme scenarios.

Table 4 and figures 12–16 display net debt interest payments as a percent of GDP in each economy. Except for the optimistic growth scenario in the euro area and the emerging markets, interest payments are rising in all economies under all scenarios. Net debt interest payments rise most dramatically in Japan, reflecting the larger growth of debt projected for Japan.

Figure 8 Effective interest rate on general government debt—Japan

percent

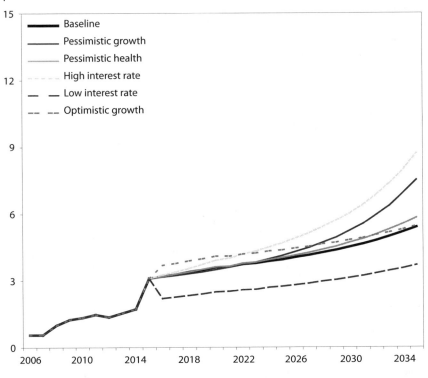

Source: Author calculations and IMF fiscal data and projections for 2005–14.

The Limits of Debt

A sovereign default by the United States or a major country in Europe is obviously unthinkable for policymakers. Nevertheless, markets can react to the possibility of such an occurrence in the long-term future. It is extremely difficult to lay down a hard and fast rule on the limits of borrowing, and the prospect for default, for economies in the modern era. Reinhart, Rogoff, and Savastano (2003)—in their study of the history of borrowing and default around the world, with a particular focus on emerging economies—have shown that economies differ sharply in the levels of debt that governments have tolerated without default. The question for the future is whether markets will continue to be more worried about a given level of debt in emerging economies than the same level of debt in advanced economies. In many emerging economies, the debt ratios at which defaults have occurred are much lower than the debt ratios that many advanced economies have sustained for decades. These

24

Figure 9   Effective interest rate on general government debt—Euro area

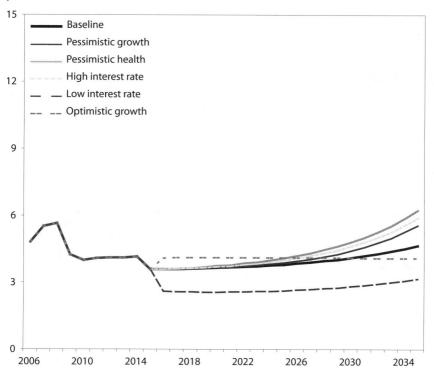

percent

Legend:
- Baseline
- Pessimistic growth
- Pessimistic health
- High interest rate
- Low interest rate
- Optimistic growth

Source: Author calculations and IMF fiscal data and projections for 2005–14.

differences in "debt intolerance" reflect the quality of institutions and the political dynamics in each economy. Reinhart, Rogoff, and Savastano argue that changes in debt intolerance happen only slowly; they point to Brazil and Chile as examples of economies with rising abilities to bear debt. Of particular interest in light of this year's fiscal stresses in Europe, they find that Greece has the lowest debt tolerance of the advanced economies covered by their study.

Ostry et al. (2010) seek to find the limits to the "tolerance" of debt in a sample of advanced economies. For each country, the estimated limit is based on the responsiveness of its fiscal policy to past changes in the level of debt. Not surprisingly, countries with a record of addressing their past problems of deficits and debts are able to run up large amounts of debt without a financial crisis. The results differ moderately across economies, but Ostry et al. find that debt ratios of around 200 percent of GDP are at the extreme limit

**Figure 10   Effective interest rate on general government debt—
Advanced economies**

percent

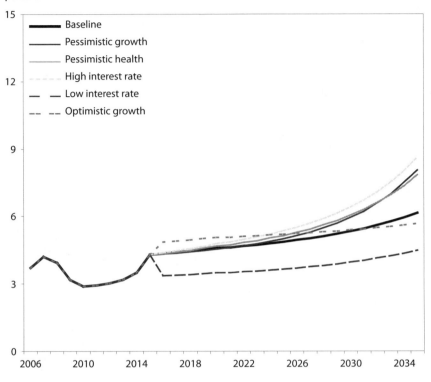

Source: Author calculations and IMF fiscal data and projections for 2005–14.

of what advanced economies can experience without becoming destabilized.[24] Their model, however, assumes that financial markets tolerate this level of debt primarily because they expect governments to take actions to reduce this burden in the future. Thus, the maximum *sustainable* level of debt is considerably lower than 200 percent of GDP.

A simple test of the plausibility of these estimated debt limits is to compare them to the historical intervals when maximum temporary and sustained debt ratios were incurred but without the expectation of default or high inflation.[25]

---

24. Ostry et al. use gross debt ratios, which range from only slightly larger than net debt ratios in some countries to considerably larger in other countries. The estimated debt ceilings for individual countries range from 150 to 260 percent of GDP.

25. We believe that the high inflation episodes of the 1970s and 1980s were caused by errors in monetary policy rather than fiscal pressures.

**Figure 11 Effective interest rate on general government debt—
Emerging economies**

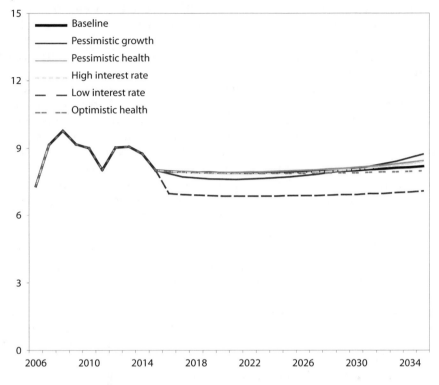

Source: Author calculations and IMF fiscal data and projections for 2005–14.

One obvious case of such tolerance is a time of war. According to CBO (2010b),
US federal net debt peaked at just over 100 percent of GDP in 1945, at the
close of World War II, and then declined steeply. According to Mares (2010),
UK public sector net debt peaked at roughly 250 percent of GDP at the ends of
the Napoleonic Wars and World War II and declined steeply after each episode.
According to Reinhart (2010) the Netherlands after the Napoleonic Wars
and France after World War I each had a peak government debt of around
250 percent of GDP which subsequently declined steeply. Special factors such
as rationing and appeals to patriotism may allow governments to run up higher
debts during wars than otherwise. But there are limits even to these circumstances. We are not aware of any episodes of net government debt ratios above
250 percent of GDP that did not lead to default or high inflation. Indeed, in
many cases—particularly among emerging markets—debt ratios much lower
than 250 percent of GDP led to default or high inflation.

Overall, 200 percent of GDP is a reasonable—perhaps even conservative—estimate of the maximum temporary net debt ratio during peacetime, at least for advanced economies. We judge the maximum sustainable level of debt to be at least 100 percent of GDP, because Belgium and Italy each have experienced periods lasting more than 10 years with net debt ratios around or above 100 percent of GDP. For most emerging markets, maximum temporary and sustainable debt ratios are likely to be substantially lower than 200 percent and 100 percent of GDP.

An alternative way of measuring the limits of debt is based on the level of net interest payments that governments can sustain indefinitely. A minimum requirement for a sustainable level of debt is that a government must raise sufficient tax revenues to pay the interest on the debt in addition to its operating expenses. In other words, a debt is sustainable in the long run only when the primary fiscal balance is not negative.[26] A higher level of debt thus increases the burden of taxes or reduces government services. According to OECD data for the advanced economies since 1980, the highest sustained share of government revenues in GDP is around 60 percent. The lowest sustained share of government spending in GDP is around 30 percent. In principle, a government could raise revenues equal to 60 percent of GDP and have spending equal to 30 percent of GDP, leaving 30 percent of GDP for net interest payments. However, such a large burden of interest payments is not likely to be sustainable because the social characteristics of countries with high government revenues are different from those with low government spending. It would likely be politically infeasible for a low-spending country to raise its revenues to 60 percent of GDP and it would be similarly unlikely for a high-taxing country to lower its spending to 30 percent of GDP. Based on available data, no advanced economy has had net debt interest payments above 12 percent of GDP in any year. Belgium and Italy each experienced more than 10 consecutive years with net debt interest payments above 9 percent of GDP. Thus, one estimate of the maximum sustainable net debt interest payments in advanced economies is roughly 10 percent of GDP.

Future projections suggest that if trends continue, governments will surpass the existing records set by OECD countries. Table 4 and figures 12–15 show that net debt interest payments are projected to exceed 10 percent of GDP in all advanced economies under some of the pessimistic scenarios. For the United States and Japan, net debt interest payments eventually exceed 10 percent of GDP under the baseline scenario. Note that the relationship between net debt interest payments and net debt ratios depends on the effective interest rate. When the effective interest rate is 10 percent, net debt interest payments of 10 percent of GDP occur with a net debt ratio of 100 percent of

---

26. This statement is correct when the interest rate on debt equals the nominal growth rate of the economy, which roughly characterizes historical data. At high levels of government debt, the interest rate is likely to exceed the growth rate of the economy and the primary balance must be positive.

Table 4 Net interest payments on government debt (percent of GDP)

	2005	2010	2015	2020	2035
United States					
Optimistic growth	2.0	1.1	3.6	4.8	9.1
Baseline	2.0	1.1	3.6	4.5	13.2
Pessimistic growth	2.0	1.1	3.6	4.3	25.6
Pessimistic health cost	2.0	1.1	3.6	4.7	25.8
High interest rates	2.0	1.1	3.6	4.8	25.0
Euro area					
Optimistic growth	2.6	2.6	2.6	2.9	2.8
Baseline	2.6	2.6	2.6	2.7	5.7
Pessimistic growth	2.6	2.6	2.6	2.7	7.7
Pessimistic health cost	2.6	2.6	2.6	2.8	12.4
High interest rates	2.6	2.6	2.6	2.7	7.7
Japan					
Optimistic growth	0.7	1.2	4.6	6.9	16.9
Baseline	0.7	1.2	4.6	6.2	19.1
Pessimistic growth	0.7	1.2	4.6	5.8	34.1
Pessimistic health cost	0.7	1.2	4.6	6.3	23.1
High interest rates	0.7	1.2	4.6	6.7	37.6
Advanced economies					
Optimistic growth	1.8	1.5	3.4	4.2	6.4
Baseline	1.8	1.5	3.4	3.9	9.9
Pessimistic growth	1.8	1.5	3.4	3.8	16.6
Pessimistic health cost	1.8	1.5	3.4	4.1	19.1
High interest rates	1.8	1.5	3.4	4.0	16.1
Emerging economies					
Optimistic growth	2.6	2.0	2.1	1.5	2.1
Baseline	2.6	2.0	2.1	1.7	2.9
Pessimistic growth	2.6	2.0	2.1	1.7	4.4
Pessimistic health cost	2.6	2.0	2.1	1.8	3.9
High interest rates	2.6	2.0	2.1	1.7	3.0

Source: Author calculations and IMF fiscal data and projections for 2005–14.

GDP. When the effective interest rate is 5 percent, net debt interest payments of 10 percent of GDP occur with a net debt ratio of 200 percent of GDP. Because 5 percent is a relatively low interest rate in historical terms, and because interest rates tend to increase with the debt ratio, it is extremely unlikely that a net debt ratio of 200 percent of GDP could be maintained indefinitely.

Figure 12   Net debt interest payments—United States

percent of GDP

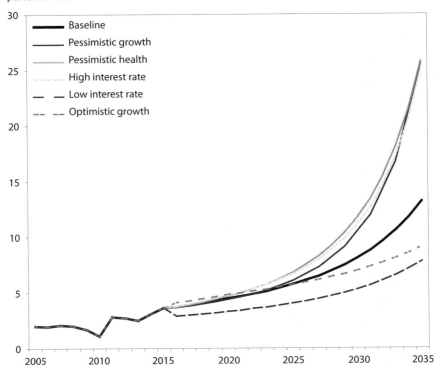

Source: Author calculations and IMF fiscal data and projections for 2005–14.

The outlook is much more hopeful for emerging economies. Figure 16 shows that the 10 percent threshold for net debt interest payments is not breached under any scenario for these economies. These lower paths reflect their much lower debt projections in aggregate. As noted above, however, many emerging economies have exhibited historical tendencies to default on debt at much lower levels than those of advanced economies. For these economies, the projected rise in the aggregate net debt ratio to nearly 60 percent of GDP by 2035 in some of the pessimistic scenarios represents a historically large increase in government debt. Moreover, these scenarios for the emerging markets may be excessively optimistic in assuming that emerging markets will not run larger fiscal deficits as their financial markets develop. Because of the greater debt intolerance of emerging markets and the risk that governments in these economies will be tempted to run larger fiscal deficits as their financial markets deepen, we do not take much comfort from projections of their debts and interest payments that are considerably lower than those in the advanced economies.

Figure 13 Net debt interest payments—Japan

percent of GDP

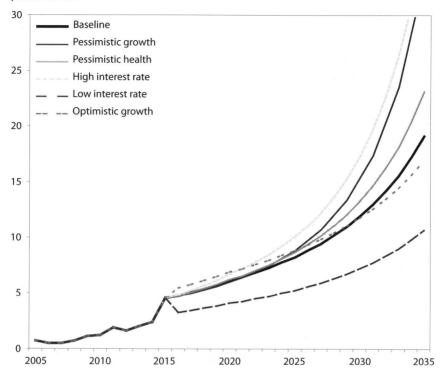

Legend:
- **Baseline**
- Pessimistic growth
- Pessimistic health
- High interest rate
- Low interest rate
- Optimistic growth

Source: Author calculations and IMF fiscal data and projections for 2005–14.

Fiscal Crises

Have Greece and Ireland provided a cautionary tale for the rest of the developed world? The sharp increase in fiscal deficits after the global financial crisis posed enormous challenges, not only for Greece and Ireland, which have gross government debt close to 100 percent of GDP, but for some other countries in the euro area as well.

As noted above, Reinhart, Rogoff, and Savastano (2003) had previously identified Greece as the advanced economy with the lowest tolerance for debt. On October 21 2009, the Greek government reported that the budget deficit for 2009 had to be revised from 3.7 percent of GDP to 12.7 percent, one of the highest among advanced countries. This announcement sparked fears that Greece might default on its debts. Interest rates began to rise on government debt of Greece and other euro-area countries that were hit hard by the collapse of the housing bubble. On March 15, 2010, the European Council set up an

Figure 14　Net debt interest payments—Euro area

percent of GDP

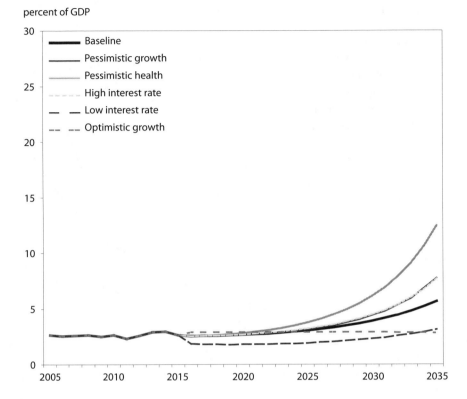

Source: Author calculations and IMF fiscal data and projections for 2005–14.

emergency mechanism to lend to members of the European Union. Faced with skyrocketing interest rates and the growing possibility that it would not be able to sell its bonds at any rate, Greece requested an emergency loan. On April 23, 2010, Greece received an initial €30 billion from this fund with participation by the IMF. The loan was later increased to €110 billion for three years. The larger package was designed to allow Greece to finance its deficit and pay off maturing debt without issuing new bonds until 2012. In return, Greece committed to an ambitious plan to cut its deficit to 8 percent of GDP in 2010 and less than 3 percent by 2014, as well as to undertake comprehensive structural reforms to boost long-run economic growth and efficiency in the public sector.

In the fall of 2010, Ireland became the focus of financial market concern, after the Irish government revealed that the cost of fixing Irish banks would raise the national debt by 21 percent of GDP. Yield spreads on Irish government debt rose further after the release of a fiscal plan that markets appear to view as overly optimistic about future Irish economic growth and tax revenues.

Figure 15 Net debt interest payments—Advanced economies

percent of GDP

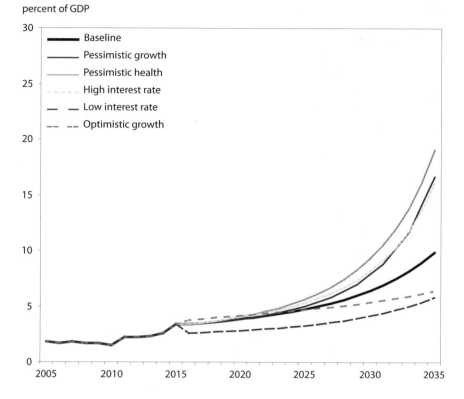

Source: Author calculations and IMF fiscal data and projections for 2005–14.

On November 21, 2010 Ireland arranged an emergency loan from the European Union and the IMF in conjunction with a 4-year fiscal austerity program. Unlike Greece, Ireland was not identified by Reinhart, Rogoff, and Savastano as a relatively debt intolerant country. The recent experiences with Greece and, especially, Ireland raise an urgent question. Could the major advanced economies experience a similar crisis, with sharply higher interest rates and the possibility of suddenly being unable to borrow in financial markets? What would be the implications for exchange rates?

As discussed above, none of the major advanced economies is close to the maximum temporary debt ratio of around 200 percent of GDP and only Japan has debt in excess of 100 percent of GDP.[27] The smooth paths of

---

27. It is possible that circumstances unique to Japan, namely a high private saving rate and a strong preference of domestic savers for domestic assets, mean that the limits to government debt are higher for Japan than for other advanced economies. However, these unique advantages are threatened by the rapid ageing of Japan's population.

Figure 16 Net debt interest payments—Emerging economies

percent of GDP

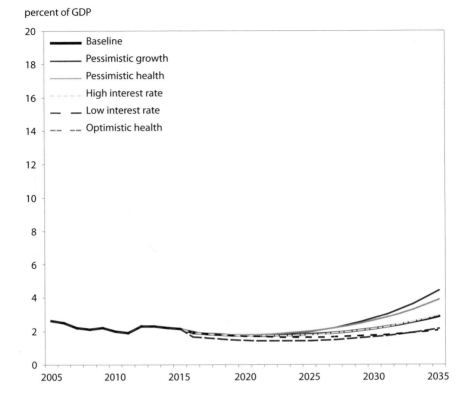

Source: Author calculations and IMF fiscal data and projections for 2005–14.

interest rates shown in figures 7–11 should not be taken as a prediction of the smoothness with which actual interest rates will evolve on current policies. These figures are based on average historical behavior, and by necessity are smooth. In reality, markets are more likely to swing quickly from under-reaction to over-reaction. As discussed above, financial markets currently appear to expect that governments will take actions over the medium term to prevent a debt explosion. Thus, long-term interest rates currently are lower than they would be if markets expected debt ratios to rise as projected in most of the scenarios shown in figures 1–6. Should financial markets come to doubt that governments will correct the problem in an orderly way, interest rates would surely rise rapidly and the prices of most financial assets would likely decline or at least become more volatile. Thus, the response of financial markets to a growing fiscal problem is likely to be discontinuous, rather than smooth. On the other hand, the extreme speed and severity with which the crises occurred in Greece and Ireland reflects circumstances that are not present in the major advanced economies.

Crises are inherently unpredictable.[28] One thing we do know is that the most extreme and sudden debt crises occur when a government cannot sell more bonds despite raising the interest rate it offers. In these extreme cases, creditors come to see higher interest rates as self-defeating because they make it harder for the government to service its debt. At this point investors refuse to buy the bonds at any interest rate. In such crisis situations, the government must suddenly choose one of three options: 1) default on its debt; 2) immediately reduce spending or increase revenues enough to service its debt; or 3) arrange a loan from other governments or international financial institutions.[29]

This sudden disruption in the ability to sell bonds does not occur when governments borrow in their own currency and when they have not committed to maintaining that currency's value in terms of other currencies. Under those conditions—which characterize each of the major advanced economies—governments can print enough money to pay off bonds at any interest rate.[30] For these economies, there may never be a single defining moment of crisis, but rather a drift into ever-higher inflation and interest rates, ever-lower growth or deeper recession, and eventually hyperinflation along with rapid currency depreciation. Most economists would view such a prospect as a progressive strangulation of a nation's wellbeing. Although a sudden Greek-style crisis is not a serious risk for the United States or other major advanced economies, the implications of a fiscal crisis are still dire.

Is it possible to have a *moderate* fiscal crisis? The answer appears to be "yes". For the major advanced economies, the most relevant examples of moderate fiscal crises are those that affected Australia and Canada in the early 1990s. Governments in these economies did not borrow in foreign currencies to a significant extent and they were not committed to maintaining fixed values of their currencies. In these episodes, real interest rates rose and economic growth stagnated over a period of months and years. Governments eventually responded by cutting primary deficits significantly and debt ratios were put on a sustainable track, thus avoiding a drift into more severe crisis.

For the major advanced economies, the most relevant examples of severe fiscal crises are the episodes that led to hyperinflation, including in Austria, Germany, Hungary, and Poland in the 1920s, and in Argentina and Brazil in the 1980s. Even in these extreme episodes, governments did not face a specific day on which wrenching change was forced upon them. Instead, their economic decline was relatively continuous—albeit accelerating. According to Sargent

---

28. Although some economists warned in the last several years that global imbalances could produce a financial crisis, the shape of the crisis that occurred was not something even many of these experts foresaw.

29. If the government is running a primary deficit at the time of the crisis, option (1) is not sufficient by itself and the primary deficit must be brought into balance.

30. Note that Greece and Ireland cannot print euros to pay their debts. Indeed, no individual member of the euro area has control over the creation of euros, but the area as a whole does have such control.

(1982), in the hyperinflations of the 1920s, accelerating inflation continuously eroded the real resources that governments could command via taxes and money creation, and economies slid deeper into recession, until eventually it became clear that a deliberate move to a new monetary and fiscal regime was the only way to avoid anarchy.

The Global Nature of the Increase in Debt

The build-up of government debt in the past few years has been widespread across advanced economies, and the long-run pressures on government budgets from ageing populations are nearly universal. In the absence of corrective action, the projected path for government debt on a global basis would be unprecedented for peacetime. Does the global nature of the looming debt build-up pose any special concerns relative to the case of a single country with a large debt? In principle, it might, but in practice the concerns do not appear to be significantly greater than those we have already described.

In a world with mobile capital, a small country can run up a large debt (relative to the size of its economy) with little effect on the rate of interest it pays, as long as markets do not doubt its ability and willingness to service that debt without resorting to inflation. By definition, a small country is one that cannot affect global markets significantly. But, if all countries run up large debts, the supply of finance in global markets will be put under strain and interest rates will rise. For this reason, a global debt increase will have larger effects on global interest rates than an increase limited to a single country.

However, for a country to run up a large debt with little effect on its own interest rates, nearly all of that debt must be held by foreigners. In the real world, capital was not highly mobile until recently, and it is only in the past decade or so that substantial fractions of each country's debt have been held by foreigners. Even now, disproportionate shares are held domestically. Between World War I and the 1980s, international capital flows were tightly restricted, and almost all of each country's debt was financed domestically. For example, the large debts incurred by the United Kingdom and the United States during World War II and the large debt incurred by Italy in the 1980s were financed almost entirely domestically.[31] Each country was isolated from capital markets in the rest of the world and thus had to bear the full effects of any debt increase on its interest rate. So the lessons we draw from the historical experiences of individual countries are, to a large extent, the lessons that are appropriate for a global debt buildup.

A recent IMF study tests for a differential effect of global versus country-specific increases in deficits on interest rates using data since 1980, when capital restrictions began to be reduced.[32] Interestingly, the study finds a signif-

---

31. The US and Canadian lend-lease programs accounted for only about 10 percent of UK debt in 1945.

32. See Baldacci and Kumar (2010). This test is conducted using deficits and not debts, presumably because the debt data are less widely available. To compare with the estimated effects of debt

icant difference between the effects of country-specific and global increases in debts. However, the results show that a global increase in debt (i.e., an increase both in the country and in the rest of the world) has an effect on interest rates at the low end of the estimates we use in this study and a country-specific increase (i.e., an increase in the country but not in the rest of the world) has an even smaller effect—about half as large.[33] On balance, it would appear that the scenarios we have constructed for each country or region have increases in interest rates that are too large for debt increases that are not shared globally and about right for debt increases that are shared globally.

These results are also consistent with the implications of the standard Cobb-Douglas model assuming a capital-income ratio of 3 and an exponent on capital of 0.35. In that case, even under the extreme assumption of complete crowding out of private investment, an increase in global net government debt from 50 percent of GDP to 100 percent of GDP would raise interest rates by 1.5 percentage points, which is slightly less than assumed in our baseline scenario. A similar increase in debt limited to a single country would have a much smaller effect.

To the extent that capital is more mobile now than in previous decades, the effect of a fiscal deficit on a country's interest rates is smaller than before but the spillovers to its neighbors are larger than before.[34] This increased spillover effect makes it all the more important for countries to work together in international forums to achieve better outcomes for the world economy. It is also important to note that even with mobile capital, a small country with a large deficit may face high interest rates if investors doubt its ability or willingness to service its debt without resorting to high inflation.

It should be noted that one of the key factors keeping interest rates low in advanced economies is the unprecedented flow of capital from governments in developing economies. According to the IMF, developing economies have added to their foreign exchange reserves at the rate of $500 billion to $1,200 billion per year in the past six years. In addition, oil exporting developing economies saved a large fraction of their net oil exports in recent years. By setting interest rates equal to growth rates in 2015, we are implicitly assuming that these flows of capital from developing economies to advanced economies will return to more normal levels. However, it is possible that these flows could fall below normal or even reverse for a while. A recent study by McKinsey and Company (Dobbs and Spence 2011) argues that developing economies are

---

described in box 1, we assume, as discussed in Baldacci and Kumar, that a one percentage point increase in the deficit is expected to lead to a 9 percentage point increase in the debt.

33. In the standard specification, which drops the rest-of-world deficit, the coefficient on the country-specific deficit is nearly as high as the sum of the coefficients on the country-specific and rest-of-world deficits in the version that includes both. This result may be due to a high degree of correlation in deficits across countries.

34. Of course, the spillover from any one country is still small.

stepping up their investment in domestic infrastructure projects and that this will push up interest rates over the long term.

Domestic versus Foreign Creditors

Does foreign ownership of sovereign debt increase the risk of a debt crisis? This is a question widely discussed in political circles, with lawmakers and presidential candidates alike warning that the United States faces an especially uncertain future because a large portion of its public debt is held by foreign governments, particularly China. But whether China or any other large holder of public debt would precipitate a crisis by selling off its holdings is highly questionable. Foreign ownership, in other words, is a complicated element in the mix of concerns about the growing indebtedness of the United States or other major countries.

The globalization of financial markets has increased the share of each country's debt that is held by foreigners. For example, 46 percent of US Treasury securities (excluding those held in government accounts) are held by foreigners.[35] As of 2009, US residents held foreign assets valued at 130 percent of US GDP and foreign residents held US assets valued at 150 percent of US GDP (IMF *International Financial Statistics* database). Thus, the United States had a negative net international investment position (NIIP) of 20 percent of GDP in 2009. Cline (2009) projects that, under fiscal assumptions fairly similar to those in our baseline scenario, the negative NIIP would grow by roughly as much as the net increase in US government debt, to 140 percent of GDP by 2030.[36] This result suggests that a large part of any increased government debt might be held by foreigners.

The foregoing analysis of debt limits and fiscal crises is not directly affected by the nationality of a government's creditors, because it is based on the behavior of the borrowing governments and not their creditors. What could be affected, however, is the willingness of borrowing governments to take actions to service their debts. For example, a high share of debt held by foreigners might deter a debtor government from inflicting higher taxes or lower spending for vital services on its populace. Just as the Irish may be reluctant to embark on such measures in order to protect German and French banks, so Americans might in some distant future resist steps demanded by investors in China. The high share of foreigners among holders of emerging-economy debt may explain in part the lower debt tolerance of many emerging economies.[37] It remains to be seen whether such an effect is significant among

---

35. Data refer to June 2010 from the US Treasury International Capital database and the US *Treasury Bulletin*.

36. The 2008 NIIP in Cline's study was –31 percent of GDP, but the data have since been revised to –24 percent for 2008 with a further narrowing in 2009 owing to valuation adjustments. Cline's study implicitly assumes that other countries do not have rising fiscal deficits.

37. Indeed, Appendix 1 in Abbas et al. (2010a) shows that in a sample of 60 advanced and emerging

the advanced economies, but it is not inconceivable that talk of "bond market vigilantes" among those protesting against budget cuts or tax increases could take on a nationalist tinge even in the developed world.

Other things equal, despite the talk in the United States and elsewhere of possible malign motives of Chinese or other debt holders, there is no reason to believe that foreign holders of a country's debt are more likely to sell in a panic than domestic holders.[38] Were China to sell off some of its US government debt out of pique or for political motivation, such a move would hurt China and its export sector even more than it might hurt the United States.[39] In their authoritative guide to recent financial crises in emerging markets, Roubini and Setser (2004) do not draw any broad distinctions in behavior between domestic and foreign creditors. Goldberg et al. (2000) find no evidence that foreign banks are more volatile lenders in local markets than domestic banks.

One notable feature of modern financial markets is that preferences of both domestic and foreign investors for assets in different currencies can swing violently for little apparent reason, leading to large changes in exchange rates. Gagnon (2009, 2010) shows that sharp exchange rate depreciations in advanced economies over the past 25 years have not been accompanied by rising bond yields or adverse economic outcomes.

Of course, the global shift in debt that pertains in the world is without precedent. The new element is the large extent to which governments in emerging economies hold the debt of governments in advanced economies, mainly as foreign exchange reserves but also in sovereign wealth funds. Many of these holdings result from currency manipulations by emerging countries like China, which keep their currencies from appreciating by making major purchases of US debt. It is too soon to tell whether these official investors will behave differently in the event of any future fiscal crisis.

The Risk of Financial Repression

Financial repression is a time-tested way for governments to hold down their borrowing costs. Repression typically operates through restrictions on the assets households and businesses can hold, especially on foreign assets.

---

economies, a higher share of domestic debt in government debt is associated with a higher sovereign rating. However, "domestic debt" is defined by the currency denomination and location of issue, not by the holder of the debt. On this definition, all US Treasury debt is domestic debt, despite the fact that nearly half is held by foreigners.

38. Altman and Haass (2010) argue that in a future political crisis with China over Taiwan, "Chinese central bankers could prove more dangerous than Chinese admirals" if they decide to cut back on their dollar holdings. As discussed below, any such action would likely hurt China more than the United States.

39. Indeed, in the present environment of falling inflation and excess capacity it is hard to see any harm to the United States from a Chinese sell-off. The primary effect of a Chinese sell-off would be to depreciate the dollar. Gagnon (2010) shows that sharp depreciations do not have harmful economic effects when a country's central bank maintains stable prices.

These restrictions funnel domestic savings into bank deposits; banks are then required to hold a given share of their assets in government bonds. In extreme cases, governments use financial repression to increase the budgetary benefits of high inflation. For example, in the early 1970s India capped bank deposit rates at 5 percent while inflation was around 20 percent (Reinhart and Rogoff, 2009, p. 143). Financial repression cannot be applied to foreign savers, however, and countries that rely heavily on foreign financing of their deficits may be less likely to turn to crudely repressive measures for fear of scaring away these lenders. Of course, if the prospects for fiscal deficits become grim enough to scare off foreign lenders anyway, then the incentive to apply repressive measures to domestic savers becomes harder to resist.

A subtler form of financial repression might occur through prudential regulation of financial institutions. The proposed Basel III rules make government bonds more attractive to banks because of the increased emphasis on asset liquidity. At the same time, the proposed Solvency II rules for insurance companies increase the risk-weighting on corporate bonds relative to government bonds. Many governments are also expected to pressure pension funds to shift the mix of equity versus bond holdings in favor of bonds, especially government bonds. On balance, these regulatory changes could increase the effective pool of capital available to governments by a substantial amount throughout the advanced economies. Indeed, recognition of these likely developments may already have put downward pressure on sovereign bond yields.

Paths to Safety

This section examines the size and timing of fiscal actions needed to restore each economy to the net debt ratio it had in 2005 by 2035. The choice to target debt ratios in 2005 is somewhat arbitrary, but it reflects a judgment that government debt in 2005 was comfortably below the long-run limits of debt and thus allows considerable room for governments to respond to future economic downturns.[40] Many observers believe that the net debt ratios in 2005 were higher than optimal in most advanced economies, but the issue of the optimal long-run level of government debt is beyond the scope of this book. Table 5 and figures 17–22 redisplay the baseline net debt paths. For each economy, two alternative paths are shown that get the ratio of net debt to GDP in 2035 back to its value in 2005. It is not the purpose of this book to outline specific courses of action on revenues or spending, and we will focus only on changes to the primary deficit.

---

40. The 2005 debt ratios are similar across economic regions except for Japan, where the ratio is higher. As discussed above, the limits of debt may be higher in Japan than in the other economies. For the United States, the 2005 debt ratio is very close to that targeted by the National Commission on Fiscal Responsibility and Reform (2010).

Table 5   Adjustment paths for general government net debt (percent of GDP)

	2010	2015	2020	2025	2030	2035
United States						
Baseline	65	86	99	120	153	213
Gradual (4.3 percent in 2016–20)	65	86	82	70	57	43
Abrupt (12.7 percent in 2026)	65	86	99	120	82	43
Euro area						
Baseline	67	73	76	85	102	133
Gradual (0.4 percent in 2016)	67	73	69	65	60	55
Abrupt (6.2 percent in 2026)	67	73	76	85	69	55
Japan						
Baseline	121	153	183	225	286	386
Gradual (11.3 percent in 2016–27)	121	153	165	152	120	85
Abrupt (23.2 percent in 2026)	121	153	183	225	157	85
Advanced economies						
Baseline	67	81	90	106	132	178
Gradual (2.6 percent in 2016–18)	67	81	76	67	58	48
Abrupt (10.0 percent in 2026)	67	81	90	106	77	48
Emerging economies						
Baseline	27	26	24	25	30	40
Gradual (–0.8 percent in 2016)	27	26	27	28	29	30
Abrupt (1.0 percent in 2026)	27	26	24	25	25	30
World						
Baseline	54	59	61	67	78	98
Gradual	54	59	54	48	43	38
Abrupt	54	59	61	67	50	38

Note: Gradual adjustment combines a discrete 1 percent per year cut in the primary deficit starting in 2016 with a permanent offset to rising pension and health care costs starting in 2016. Abrupt adjustment assumes a one-time discrete cut in 2026.

Source: Author calculations and IMF fiscal data and projections for 2005–14.

Gradual (Early) Adjustment

The first set of paths, labeled "Gradual," consists of a sequence of cumulative reductions in the primary deficit by 1 percent a year beginning in 2016 coupled with an elimination of the trend increases in pension and health care deficits in

Figure 17 Adjustment paths for general government debt—United States

percent of GDP

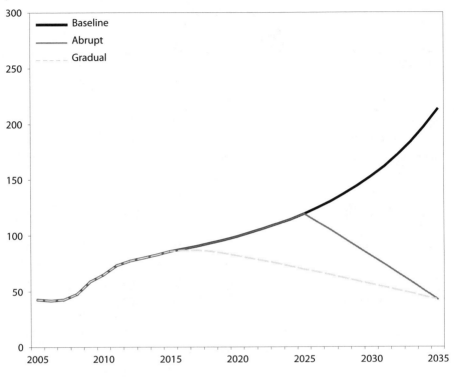

Source: Author calculations and IMF fiscal data and projections for 2005–14.

the years 2016–35.[41] The reductions do not start before 2016 because primary deficits are already projected to be declining significantly through 2015 as fiscal stimulus measures run off, governments implement current plans for fiscal cuts, and economic recovery boosts revenues.[42] Additional budget cuts in the next two or three years would threaten the durability of the recovery. However, in the case of Japan, the IMF projects relatively little reduction in primary deficits between 2010 and 2015, and thus additional cuts might usefully be

41. The trend increases could be reduced, for example, by linking the retirement age to average longevity and linking health-care program revenues to health-care costs. Abbas et al. (2010a) show that raising the retirement age 1½ years would be sufficient to stabilize public pension expenditure in EU countries over the next 20 years. The National Commission on Fiscal Responsibility and Reform (2010) discusses other options to stabilize these costs.

42. As discussed previously, achieving the IMF projected primary deficits in 2015 requires that governments follow through on current plans to cut deficits, many of which have not yet been enacted into law.

Figure 18 Adjustment paths for general government debt—Japan

percent of GDP

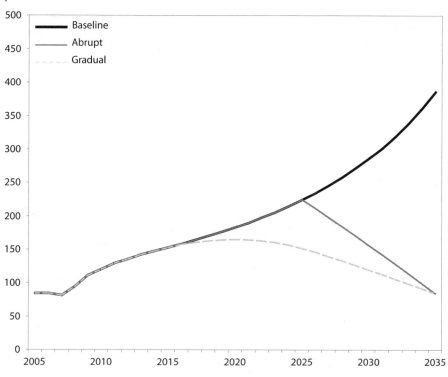

Source: Author calculations and IMF fiscal data and projections for 2005–14.

implemented in 2014 and 2015. We did not insert additional earlier cuts in these adjustment scenarios for Japan in order to keep the treatment comparable across countries and because the long-run effects of slightly earlier cuts are not large. The magnitude of the annual cuts (1 percent of GDP) is designed to allow for a relatively smooth transition, but making cuts of this magnitude nevertheless requires difficult choices for a society and its leaders.

The sequence of discrete budget cuts is assumed to last as long as needed to achieve the target debt ratio in 2035.[43] For the United States, the primary deficit must be cut 1 percentage point per year for 4.3 years, for a total cut of 4.3 percent of GDP. For the euro area, the sequence lasts 0.4 years. For Japan, it lasts 11.3 years. For the advanced economies in aggregate, it lasts 2.6 years. For the emerging economies, no discrete budget cuts are needed as long as the net costs of future pension and health care benefits are stabilized.

---

43. For computational reasons, this scenario does not include a positive feedback from faster GDP growth to lower primary deficits, so these magnitudes of adjustment are conservative.

Figure 19   Adjustment paths for general government debt—Euro area

percent of GDP

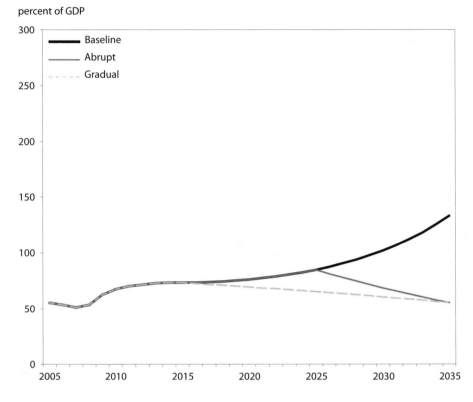

Baseline
Abrupt
Gradual

Source: Author calculations and IMF fiscal data and projections for 2005–14.

Abrupt (Delayed) Adjustment

The second set of paths, labeled "Abrupt," assumes that no action is taken until 2026, at which time there is a large permanent cut in the primary deficit. This scenario might arise as the result of a fiscal crisis. Of course, even in a crisis it might not be necessary or even feasible to make the budget cuts all in one year, so this scenario should not be taken too literally. The point is that delaying adjustment is likely to require future cuts that are both larger and more abrupt. For the United States, the delayed cut is nearly 13 percent of GDP. For the euro area, it is 6 percent of GDP. For Japan, it is a whopping 23 percent of GDP. For the advanced economies in aggregate, it is 10 percent of GDP. For the emerging economies, it is a modest 1 percent of GDP.

For the advanced economies, these abrupt budget cuts would be enormously disruptive. In the United States, for example, a budget cut of nearly 13 percent of GDP in 2025 could be achieved by eliminating all federal

Figure 20   Adjustment paths for general government debt—Advanced economies

percent of GDP

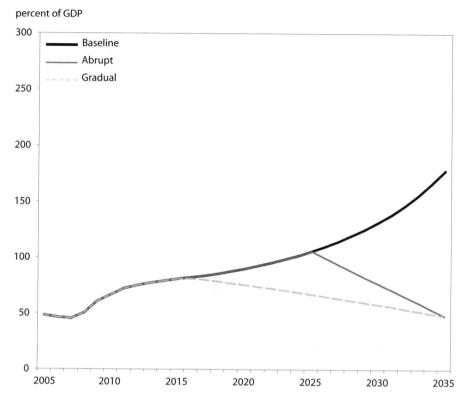

Source: Author calculations and IMF fiscal data and projections for 2005–14.

spending on Social Security, Medicare, Medicaid, and other health programs or by increasing all federal taxes by 55 percent.

Benefits of Early and Gradual Adjustment

Both the gradual and the abrupt adjustment are associated with lower interest rates after 2025 than in the baseline scenario. In part because of these reductions in interest rates, GDP growth picks up in both adjustment scenarios.[44] But these benefits kick in much earlier under the gradual adjustment scenario and they result in a level of US GDP that is 5 percent higher by 2035 than in

---

44. Neither scenario includes any negative short-run effect of fiscal cuts on GDP. This assumption is plausible for pre-announced gradual cuts but is surely too optimistic for the abrupt adjustment scenario.

Figure 21   Adjustment paths for general government debt—Emerging economies

percent of GDP

Source: Author calculations and IMF fiscal data and projections for 2005–14.

the abrupt adjustment scenario and 15 percent higher than in the baseline. For Japan, gradual adjustment raises 2035 GDP by 13 percent relative to baseline, and in the euro area 2035 GDP is 6 percent higher than in the baseline. In addition to a lower path of interest rates and faster GDP growth, the gradual adjustment scenario minimizes the risk of crisis because it prevents the build-up of debt that occurs under the abrupt scenario.

Another important benefit is that gradual adjustment announced well in advance allows citizens time to plan and adjust smoothly. For example, in the 1983 reforms to the US Social Security pension system, tax increases were phased in over 7 years and future increases in the retirement age did not affect any worker within 20 years of retiring under the existing system.[45] Giving citi-

---

45. See the Social Security Administration website at http://www.ssa.gov/history/1983amend.html.

Figure 22 Adjustment paths for general government debt—World

percent of GDP

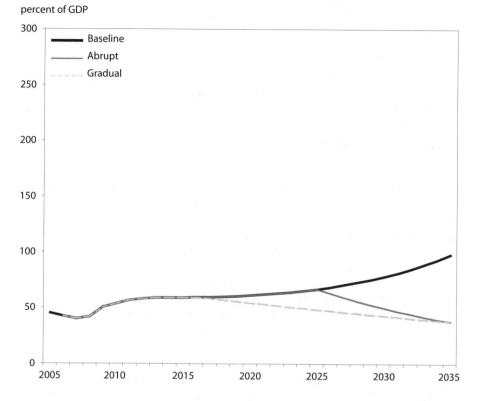

Source: Author calculations and IMF fiscal data and projections for 2005–14.

zens time to plan is a powerful motivation for enacting the necessary long-run fiscal adjustment now, even though implementation would not begin for several years.

Differential Speeds of Adjustment across Economies

Because we now live with a global capital market, it is more important than before to coordinate fiscal adjustment. In particular, as highlighted by the Leaders of the G-20, a simultaneous and premature fiscal consolidation could be harmful because global aggregate demand currently is below potential aggregate supply. Economies operating below potential should hold off adjustment in the near term (although they should adopt specific plans for future adjustment). In order to support global economic recovery and avoid widening global imbalances, economies with current account surpluses should delay fiscal adjustment longer than economies with current account deficits.

As the global recovery strengthens and economies approach potential, interest rates are likely to rise. What are the prospects for an economy that does not tackle its fiscal problems over the medium run when other economies do? There are two offsetting considerations: On the one hand, fiscal laggards may benefit from a dampened increase in global interest rates when most other countries undertake substantial fiscal consolidation. On the other hand, fiscal laggards may have difficulty maintaining financial market confidence when investors have the option to hold debt issued by many other countries with sound fiscal positions.

What Promotes Adjustment?

There are obvious incentives to act early even before crises occur. Guichard et al. (2007) study episodes of major fiscal consolidations in OECD countries since the late 1970s. They ask the following questions: 1) What causes governments to embark on fiscal consolidation? 2) What determines the speed and ultimate amount of consolidation? 3) What causes governments to terminate consolidation? And 4) what factors make consolidations more likely to succeed in stabilizing the debt ratio?

They find that each percentage point increase in the cyclically adjusted primary deficit increases the odds that a country will start fiscal consolidation by 5 percentage points. Each percentage point increase in interest rates relative to the rest of the world increases the odds of starting fiscal consolidation by 1 percentage point. And the odds of starting fiscal consolidation rise by 14 percentage points immediately after an election.[46] They also find that higher initial cyclically adjusted primary deficits and higher interest rates have large positive effects on the size and speed of fiscal consolidation. The strength or weakness of the economy has little effect on the likelihood of starting a consolidation, but consolidations are much slower and more likely to be terminated when the economy is weak. Consolidations are more likely to succeed in stabilizing the debt when they focus on cutting social spending and are accompanied by explicit rules limiting spending or deficits. Somewhat surprisingly, strong economic activity at the start of the consolidation significantly reduces the odds of success in stabilizing the debt ratio.

Alesina and Ardagna (2009) find that fiscal consolidations based mainly on spending reductions rather than tax increases are more likely to succeed in reducing the debt ratio, in part because they are less likely to reduce economic growth. Indeed, they identify many episodes in which consolidation achieved largely through spending cuts led to faster economic growth. The finding

---

46. Interestingly, Alesina, Carloni, and Lecce (2010) find that large fiscal consolidations do not significantly affect the probability of the governing party losing the next election. In a study of fiscal consolidations in eastern European economies over the past two years, Åslund (2010) shows that very aggressive fiscal cuts were politically acceptable, perhaps because of the rapid increase in real incomes immediately prior to the crisis.

that spending cuts are more effective than tax increases likely depends importantly on the fact that most of the countries examined had high initial ratios of spending to GDP and it may not apply to countries with low levels of spending. Jayadev and Konczal (2010) point out that the episodes identified by Alesina and Ardagna in which consolidation led to faster growth almost never began during or soon after a recession. The sole exception was Ireland in 1987, which benefited from a large depreciation in its exchange rate, sharply lower interest rates, and rapid growth in its main export market, the United Kingdom. IMF (2010b) revisits this issue using a new method to identify exogenous fiscal actions and finds that both spending cuts and tax increases reduce GDP growth in the short run while raising the level of GDP in the long run. This study finds that fiscal consolidations also have significant negative spillovers on trading partner growth in the short run.

Can institutionalized fiscal rules and procedures promote adjustment? Such rules are supposed to address the problem of the time inconsistency of the budget process, which arises when incumbent governments attach too much weight to the near-term benefits of tax cuts and spending increases and not enough weight to the long-term social costs of deficits. According to Lienert (2010), at a minimum fiscal rules or procedures should include medium-term fiscal objectives, a strategy for attaining these objectives in the budget process, the regular publication of reports on the attainment of fiscal objectives, and audited annual financial statements. Examples of fiscal rules and procedures include deficit rules (e.g., as established in the Stability and Growth Pact of the euro area), expenditure ceilings, and the establishment of independent fiscal councils.

The evidence on the effectiveness of fiscal rules and procedures is mixed. OECD (2010b) argues that fiscal rules can increase the likelihood of a successful and sustained consolidation. Caceres, Corbacho, and Medina (2010b), however, find that in most cases, the introduction of a fiscal responsibility law did not have any additional positive effect on fiscal consolidation programs that were already under way.

Conclusion

The run-up in government debt in response to the global financial crisis is unprecedented for peacetime. This massive increase in public debt has provided a counterweight that very likely averted a Great Depression while households and businesses deleveraged and restructured their balance sheets quickly. However, the current trajectory of fiscal policy around the world is not sustainable.

The major economies are not likely to face serious debt-related problems in the next 5 to 10 years, but all face very difficult policy choices within the next 25 years.[47] Although there is time to make these choices, time is not on our

---

47. A recent report by Standard & Poor's (Mrsnik et al. 2010, p. 2) concludes that "[t]hrough the next decade, governments likely have some breathing space as we expect pressure from age-related

side. The benefits of early planning and phased adjustment are considerable. Failure to tackle these fiscal problems in a timely manner will lead to rising interest rates and an eventual slowdown in the rate of economic growth. In most advanced economies and some developing economies, failure to act probably will result in a fiscal crisis of some form in the next 25 years. Uncertainty about the timing or nature of a potential crisis is not an excuse to do nothing.

The current weak state of many economies argues against implementing budget cuts in the next couple of years, but now is the moment to adopt concrete plans to return public finances to sound conditions over the medium term. The longer decisions are delayed, the more costly will be the ultimate adjustment and the greater the risk of a damaging economic crisis.

spending will remain relatively moderate over this period. Nevertheless, while this window to implement fiscal sustainability strategies remains open, it will not be for long with the expected acceleration in spending starting in 2020."

References

Abbas, S. M. A., O. Basdevant, S. Eble, G. Everaert, J. Gottschalk, F. Hasanov, J. Park, C. Sancak, R. Velloso, and M. Villafuerte. 2010a. *Strategies for Fiscal Consolidation in the Post-Crisis World*. Washington: International Monetary Fund Fiscal Affairs Department.

Abbas, S. M. A., N. Belhocine, A. ElGanainy, and M. Horton. 2010b. *A Historical Public Debt Database*. IMF Working Paper (WP/10/245). Washington: International Monetary Fund.

Alesina, A., and S. Ardagna. 2009. *Large Changes in Fiscal Policy: Taxes versus Spending*. NBER Working Paper 15438. Cambridge, MA: National Bureau of Economic Research.

Alesina, A., D. Carloni, and G. Lecce. 2010. *The Electoral Consequences of Large Fiscal Adjustments*. Posted at www.voxeu.org, May 29.

Altman, R., and R. Haass. 2010. American Profligacy and American Power: The Consequences of Fiscal Irresponsibility. *Foreign Affairs* (November/December).

Ardagna, S., F. Caselli, and T. Lane. 2004. *Fiscal Discipline and the Cost of Public Debt Service: Some Estimates for OECD Countries*. ECB Working Paper Series 411. Frankfurt: European Central Bank.

Åslund, A. 2010. *The Last Shall Be the First: The East European Financial Crisis, 2008–10*. Washington: Peterson Institute for International Economics.

Baldacci, E., and M. S. Kumar. 2010. *Fiscal Deficits, Public Debt, and Sovereign Bond Yields*. IMF Working Paper (WP/10/184). Washington: International Monetary Fund.

Baldacci, E., S. Gupta and A. Mati. 2008. *Political and Fiscal Risk Determinants of Sovereign Spreads in Emerging Markets*. IMF Working Paper (WP/08/259). Washington: International Monetary Fund.

Bayoumi, T., M. Goldstein and G. Woglom. 1995. Do Credit Markets Discipline Sovereign Borrowers? Evidence from US States. *Journal of Money, Credit and Banking* 27, no. 4: 1046–59.

Caceres, C., V. Guzzo, and M. Segoviano. 2010a. *Sovereign Spreads: Global Risk Aversion, Contagion or Fundamentals?* IMF Working Paper (WP/10/120). Washington: International Monetary Fund.

Caceres, C., A. Corbacho, and L. Medina. 2010b. *Structural Breaks in Fiscal Performance: Did Fiscal Responsibility Laws Have Anything to Do with Them?* IMF Working Paper (WP/10/248). Washington: International Monetary Fund.

Caner, M., T. Grennes and F. Koehler-Geib. 2010. *Finding the Tipping Point—When Sovereign Debt Turns Bad.* World Bank Policy Research Working Paper (WPS5391). Washington: World Bank.

CBO (Congressional Budget Office). 2010a. *The Long-Term Budget Outlook* (June). Washington.

CBO (Congressional Budget Office). 2010b. *Federal Debt and the Risk of a Fiscal Crisis* (July). Washington.

CBO (Congressional Budget Office). 2010c. *The Budget and Economic Outlook: An Update* (August). Washington.

CBO (Congressional Budget Office). 2011. *The Budget and Economic Outlook: Fiscal Years 2011 to 2021* (January). Washington.

Checherita, C., and P. Rother. 2010. *The Impact of High and Growing Government Debt on Economic Growth: An Empirical Investigation for the Euro Area.* ECB Working Paper no. 1237. Frankfurt: European Central Bank.

Chinn, M., and J. Frankel. 2007. *Debt and Interest Rates: The U.S. and the Euro Area.* Economics Discussion Papers (2007–11).

Cline, W. R. 2009. Long-Term Fiscal Imbalances, US External Liabilities, and Future Living Standards. In *The Long-Term International Economic Position of the United States*, ed. C. Fred Bergsten. Special Report 20. Washington: Peterson Institute for International Economics.

Conway, P., and A. Orr. 2002. *The GIRM: A Global Interest Rate Model.* Westpac Institutional Bank Occasional Paper. Wellington: Westpac Institutional Bank.

Cottarelli, C., and A. Schaechter. 2010. *Long-Term Trends in Public Finances in the G-7 Economies.* IMF Staff Position Note SPN/10/13. Washington: International Monetary Fund.

Dobbs, R., and M. Spence. 2011. The Era of Cheap Capital Draws to a Close. *McKinsey Quarterly* (February).

Dötz, N., and C. Fischer. 2010. *What Can EMU Countries' Sovereign Bond Spreads Tell us about Market Perceptions of Default Probabilities During the Recent Financial Crisis?* Discussion Paper, Series 1: Economic Studies No. 11/2010. Frankfurt: Deutsche Bundesbank.

Engen, E. M., and R. G. Hubbard. 2005. Federal Government Debt and Interest Rates. *NBER Macroeconomics Annual 2004*, no. 19: 83–138. Cambridge, MA: National Bureau of Economic Research.

Feldstein, M. 2010. *Preventing a National Debt Explosion.* NBER Working Paper 16451. Cambridge, MA: National Bureau of Economic Research.

Faini, R. 2006. Fiscal Policy and Interest Rates in Europe. *Economic Policy* 21: 443–89.

G-20 Toronto Summit Declaration. 2010. University of Toronto G20 Information Centre. Available at www.g20.utoronto.ca.

Gagnon, J. 2009. Currency Crashes and Bond Yields in Industrial Countries. *Journal of International Money and Finance* 28: 161–81.

Gagnon, J. 2010. Currency Crashes in Industrial Countries: What Determines Good and Bad Outcomes? *International Finance* 13, no. 2: 165–94.

Gale, W. G., and P. R. Orszag. 2004. Budget Deficits, National Saving, and Interest Rates. *Brookings Papers on Economic Activity* no. 2. Washington: Brookings Institution.

Goldberg, L., B. Dages, and D. Kinney. 2000. *Foreign and Domestic Bank Participation in Emerging Markets: Lessons from Mexico and Argentina.* NBER Working Paper 7714. Cambridge, MA: National Bureau of Economic Research.

Gruber, J., and S. Kamin 2010. *Fiscal Positions and Government Bond Yields in OECD Countries.* International Finance Discussion Papers no. 1012. Board of Governors of the Federal Reserve System.

Guichard, S., M. Kennedy, E. Wurzel, and C. Andre. 2007. *What Promotes Fiscal Consolidation: OECD Country Experiences.* OECD Economics Department Working Paper 553. Paris: Organization for Economic Cooperation and Development.

Haugh, D., P. Ollivaud and D. Turner. 2009. *What Drives Sovereign Risk Premiums? An Analysis of Recent Evidence from the Euro Area.* OECD Economics Department Working Papers no. 718. Paris: Organization for Economic Cooperation and Development.

Hauner, D., and M. S. Kumar. 2006. *Fiscal Policy and Interest Rates: How Sustainable is The "New Economy"?* IMF Working Paper (WP/06/112). Washington: International Monetary Fund.

Huntley, J. 2010. *Federal Debt and the Risk of a Fiscal Crisis.* Economic and Budget Issue Brief, July 27. Washington: Congressional Budget Office.

IMF (International Monetary Fund). 2010a. *From Stimulus to Consolidation: Revenue and Expenditure Policies in Advanced and Emerging Economies.* Washington: International Monetary Fund, Fiscal Affairs Department (April 30).

IMF (International Monetary Fund). 2010b. Will It Hurt? Macroeconomic Effects of Fiscal Consolidation. Chapter 3 of *World Economic Outlook* (October). Washington.

IMF (International Monetary Fund). 2010c. Fiscal Exit: From Strategy to Implementation. *Fiscal Monitor* (November). Washington.

IMF (International Monetary Fund). 2010d. *Macro-Fiscal Implications of Health Care Reform in Advanced and Emerging Economies* (December). Washington.

IMF (International Monetary Fund). 2011. *Fiscal Monitor Update* (January). Washington.

Irons, J., and J. Bivens. 2010. *Government Debt and Economic Growth: Overreaching Claims of Debt "Threshold" Suffer from Theoretical and Empirical Flaws.* EPI Briefing Paper 271. Washington: Economic Policy Institute.

Jayadev, A., and M. Konczal. 2010. *The Boom Not the Slump: The Right Time for Austerity.* Roosevelt Institute.

Kinoshita, N. 2006. *Government Debt and Long-Term Interest Rate.* IMF Working Paper (WP/06/63). Washington: International Monetary Fund.

Kitchen, J., and M. D. Chinn. 2010. *Financing US Debt: Is There Enough Money in the World— and At What Cost?* La Follette School Working Paper 2010-015. University of Wisconsin.

Kumar, M. S., and J. Woo. 2010. *Public Debt and Growth.* IMF Working Paper (WP/10/174). Washington: International Monetary Fund.

Laubach, T. 2009. New Evidence on the Interest Rate Effects of Budget Deficits and Debt. *Journal of the European Economic Association* 7, no. 4: 858-85.

Leeper, E.M. 2010. Monetary Science, Fiscal Alchemy. Paper presented at the 2010 Economic Policy Symposium, Jackson Hole. Federal Reserve Bank of Kansas City.

Lienert. I. 2010. *Should Advanced Countries Adopt a Fiscal Responsibility Law?* IMF Working Paper WP/10/254. Washington: International Monetary Fund.

Lupton, J., and D. Hensley. 2010. *Government Debt Sustainability in the Age of Fiscal Activism.* JPMorgan Chase Bank Economic Research, June 11.

Mares, A. 2010. Ask Not Whether Governments Will Default, but How. *Sovereign Subjects.* Morgan Stanley Research, August 25.

Moody's Investors Service. 2011. *Evolution of Moody's Perspective on the US Rating.* Released January 27 at www.moody's.com.

Mrsnik, M., D. T. Beers, and I. Morozov. 2010. *Global Aging 2010: An Irreversible Truth.* Standard & Poor's Global Credit Portal RatingsDirect, October 7.

National Commission on Fiscal Responsibility and Reform. 2010. T*he Moment of Truth* (December). Available at www.fiscalcommission.gov.

OECD (Organization for Economic Cooperation and Development). 2010a. *Economic Outlook 2010/1.* Paris.

OECD (Organization for Economic Cooperation and Development). 2010b. *Economic Outlook 2010/2.* Paris.

Ostry, J. D., A. R. Ghosh, J. I. Kim, and M. S. Qureshi. 2010. *Fiscal Space.* IMF Staff Position Note SPN/10/11. Washington: International Monetary Fund.

Prasad, E., and M. Ding. 2010. *The Rising Burden of Government Debt.* Washington: Global Economy and Development Program at the Brookings Institution.

Reinhart, C.M. 2010. *This Time Is Different Chartbook: Country Histories on Debt, Default, and Financial Crises.* NBER Working Paper 15815. Cambridge, MA: National Bureau of Economic Research.

Reinhart, C. M., and K. S. Rogoff. 2009. *This Time is Different: Eight Centuries of Financial Folly.* Princeton University Press.

Reinhart, C. M., and K. S. Rogoff. 2010. *Growth in a Time of Debt.* NBER Working Paper 15639. Cambridge, MA: National Bureau of Economic Analysis.

Reinhart, C. M., K. S. Rogoff, and M. A. Savastano. 2003. *Debt Intolerance.* Brookings Papers on Economic Activity no. 1: 1–62. Washington: Brookings Institution.

Roubini, N., and B. Setser. 2004. *Bailouts or Bail-ins? Responding to Financial Crises in Emerging Economies.* Washington: Institute for International Economics.

Sargent, T. J. 1982. The Ends of Four Big Inflations. In *Inflation: Causes and Effects*, ed. R. E. Hall. University of Chicago Press.

Schuknecht, L., J. von Hagen and G. Wolswijk. 2009. Government Risk Premiums in the Bond Market: EMU and Canada. *European Journal of Political Economy*, no. 25.

Sgherri, S., and E. Zoli. 2009. *Euro Area Sovereign Risk During the Crisis.* IMF Working Paper (WP/09/222). Washington: International Monetary Fund.

Warnock, F. E. 2010. How Dangerous is US Government Debt? The Risks of a Sudden Spike in US Interest Rates. *Capital Flows Quarterly* (2010Q2). Council on Foreign Relations.

About the Authors

Joseph E. Gagnon, senior fellow since September 2009, was visiting associate director, Division of Monetary Affairs (2008–09) at the US Federal Reserve Board. Previously he served at the US Federal Reserve Board as associate director, Division of International Finance (1999–2008), and senior economist (1987–90 and 1991–97). He has also served at the US Treasury Department (1994–95 and 1997–99) and has taught at the University of California's Haas School of Business (1990–91). He has published numerous articles in economics journals, including the *Journal of International Economics*, the *Journal of Monetary Economics*, the *Review of International Economics*, and the *Journal of International Money and Finance*, and has contributed to several edited volumes. He received a BA from Harvard University in 1981 and a PhD in economics from Stanford University in 1987.

Marc Hinterschweiger has been a research analyst with the Peterson Institute since 2008. He is also a PhD candidate in economics at Ludwig-Maximilians University (LMU) in Munich, Germany. His research focuses on the transmission mechanism of monetary policy, asset prices, and financial crises. He previously worked at the Rhenish-Westfalian Institute for Economic Research (RWI) in Essen, Germany. He holds a BA in economics (2005) and a BA in international affairs (2006) from the University of St. Gallen, Switzerland. He earned a master's degree in public policy from Harvard University's Kennedy School of Government (2008), where he was a McCloy scholar, specializing in international trade and finance. He has been a member of the German National Academic Foundation (Studienstiftung des deutschen Volkes) since 2002.

Index

Other Publications from the Peterson Institute for International Economics

88 **Capitalizing on the Morocco-US Free Trade Agreement: A Road Map for Success** Gary Clyde Hufbauer and Claire Brunel, eds
September 2009 ISBN 978-0-88132-433-4

89 **Three Threats: An Analytical Framework for the CFIUS Process** Theodore H. Moran
August 2009 ISBN 978-0-88132-429-7

90 **Reengaging Egypt: Options for US-Egypt Economic Relations** Barbara Kotschwar and Jeffrey J. Schott
January 2010 ISBN 978-088132-439-6

91 **Figuring Out the Doha Round** Gary Clyde Hufbauer, Jeffrey J. Schott, and Woan Foong Wong
June 2010 ISBN 978-088132-503-4

92 **China's Strategy to Secure Natural Resources: Risks, Dangers, and Opportunities** Theodore H. Moran
June 2010 ISBN 978-088132-512-6

93 **The Implications of China-Taiwan Economic Liberalization** Daniel H. Rosen and Zhi Wang
January 2011 ISBN 978-0-88132-501-0

94 **The Global Outlook for Government Debt over the Next 25 Years: Implications for the Economy and Public Policy** Joseph E. Gagnon with Marc Hinterschweiger
June 2011 *ISBN 978-0-88132-621-5*

BOOKS

IMF Conditionality* John Williamson, ed.
1983 ISBN 0-88132-006-4

Trade Policy in the 1980s* William R. Cline, ed.
1983 ISBN 0-88132-031-5

Subsidies in International Trade* Gary Clyde Hufbauer and Joanna Shelton Erb
1984 ISBN 0-88132-004-8

International Debt: Systemic Risk and Policy Response* William R. Cline
1984 ISBN 0-88132-015-3

Trade Protection in the United States: 31 Case Studies* Gary Clyde Hufbauer, Diane E. Berliner, and Kimberly Ann Elliott
1986 ISBN 0-88132-040-4

Toward Renewed Economic Growth in Latin America* Bela Balassa, Gerardo M. Bueno, Pedro Pablo Kuczynski, and Mario Henrique Simonsen
1986 ISBN 0-88132-045-5

Capital Flight and Third World Debt* Donald R. Lessard and John Williamson, eds.
1987 ISBN 0-88132-053-6

The Canada-United States Free Trade Agreement: The Global Impact* Jeffrey J. Schott and Murray G. Smith, eds.
1988 ISBN 0-88132-073-0

World Agricultural Trade: Building a Consensus* William M. Miner and Dale E. Hathaway, eds.
1988 ISBN 0-88132-071-3

Japan in the World Economy* Bela Balassa and Marcus Noland
1988 ISBN 0-88132-041-2

America in the World Economy: A Strategy for the 1990s* C. Fred Bergsten
1988 ISBN 0-88132-089-7

Managing the Dollar: From the Plaza to the Louvre* Yoichi Funabashi
1988, 2d ed. 1989 ISBN 0-88132-097-8

United States External Adjustment and the World Economy* William R. Cline
May 1989 ISBN 0-88132-048-X

Free Trade Areas and U.S. Trade Policy* Jeffrey J. Schott, ed.
May 1989 ISBN 0-88132-094-3

Dollar Politics: Exchange Rate Policymaking in the United States* I. M. Destler and C. Randall Henning
September 1989 ISBN 0-88132-079-X

Latin American Adjustment: How Much Has Happened?* John Williamson, ed.
April 1990 ISBN 0-88132-125-7

The Future of World Trade in Textiles and Apparel* William R. Cline
1987, 2d ed. June 1999 ISBN 0-88132-110-9

Completing the Uruguay Round: A Results-Oriented Approach to the GATT Trade Negotiations* Jeffrey J. Schott, ed.
September 1990 ISBN 0-88132-130-3

Economic Sanctions Reconsidered (2 volumes)
Economic Sanctions Reconsidered: Supplemental Case Histories Gary Clyde Hufbauer, Jeffrey J. Schott, and Kimberly Ann Elliott
1985, 2d ed. Dec. 1990 ISBN cloth 0-88132-115-X
ISBN paper 0-88132-105-2

Economic Sanctions Reconsidered: History and Current Policy Gary Clyde Hufbauer, Jeffrey J. Schott, and Kimberly Ann Elliott
December 1990 ISBN cloth 0-88132-140-0
ISBN paper 0-88132-136-2

Pacific Basin Developing Countries: Prospects for the Future* Marcus Noland
January 1991 ISBN cloth 0-88132-141-9
ISBN paper 0-88132-081-1

Currency Convertibility in Eastern Europe* John Williamson, ed.
October 1991 ISBN 0-88132-128-1

International Adjustment and Financing: The Lessons of 1985-1991* C. Fred Bergsten, ed.
January 1992 ISBN 0-88132-112-5

North American Free Trade: Issues and Recommendations* Gary Clyde Hufbauer and Jeffrey J. Schott
April 1992 ISBN 0-88132-120-6

Narrowing the U.S. Current Account Deficit* Alan J. Lenz
June 1992 ISBN 0-88132-103-6

The Economics of Global Warming William R. Cline
June 1992 ISBN 0-88132-132-X

Leadership Selection in the Major Multilaterals
Miles Kahler
November 2001   ISBN 0-88132-335-7

**The International Financial Architecture:
What's New? What's Missing?**   Peter B. Kenen
November 2001   ISBN 0-88132-297-0

**Delivering on Debt Relief: From IMF Gold to a
New Aid Architecture**   John Williamson and
Nancy Birdsall, with Brian Deese
April 2002   ISBN 0-88132-331-4

**Imagine There's No Country: Poverty,
Inequality, and Growth in the Era of
Globalization**   Surjit S. Bhalla
September 2002   ISBN 0-88132-348-9

Reforming Korea's Industrial Conglomerates
Edward M. Graham
January 2003   ISBN 0-88132-337-3

**Industrial Policy in an Era of Globalization:
Lessons from Asia**   Marcus Noland and
Howard Pack
March 2003   ISBN 0-88132-350-0

Reintegrating India with the World Economy
T. N. Srinivasan and Suresh D. Tendulkar
March 2003   ISBN 0-88132-280-6

**After the Washington Consensus: Restarting
Growth and Reform in Latin America**
Pedro-Pablo Kuczynski and John Williamson, eds.
March 2003   ISBN 0-88132-347-0

**The Decline of US Labor Unions and the Role
of Trade**   Robert E. Baldwin
June 2003   ISBN 0-88132-341-1

**Can Labor Standards Improve under
Globalization?**   Kimberly Ann Elliott and
Richard B. Freeman
June 2003   ISBN 0-88132-332-2

**Crimes and Punishments? Retaliation under
the WTO**   Robert Z. Lawrence
October 2003   ISBN 0-88132-359-4

Inflation Targeting in the World Economy
Edwin M. Truman
October 2003   ISBN 0-88132-345-4

**Foreign Direct Investment and Tax
Competition**   John H. Mutti
November 2003   ISBN 0-88132-352-7

**Has Globalization Gone Far Enough? The
Costs of Fragmented Markets**
Scott C. Bradford and Robert Z. Lawrence
February 2004   ISBN 0-88132-349-7

**Food Regulation and Trade: Toward a Safe and
Open Global System**   Tim Josling,
Donna Roberts, and David Orden
March 2004   ISBN 0-88132-346-2

**Controlling Currency Mismatches in Emerging
Markets**   Morris Goldstein and Philip Turner
April 2004   ISBN 0-88132-360-8

**Free Trade Agreements: US Strategies and
Priorities**   Jeffrey J. Schott, ed.
April 2004   ISBN 0-88132-361-6

Trade Policy and Global Poverty
William R. Cline
June 2004   ISBN 0-88132-365-9

**Bailouts or Bail-ins? Responding to Financial
Crises in Emerging Economies**
Nouriel Roubini and Brad Setser
August 2004   ISBN 0-88132-371-3

Transforming the European Economy
Martin Neil Baily and Jacob Funk Kirkegaard
September 2004   ISBN 0-88132-343-8

**Chasing Dirty Money: The Fight Against
Money Laundering**   Peter Reuter and
Edwin M. Truman
November 2004   ISBN 0-88132-370-5

**The United States and the World Economy:
Foreign Economic Policy for the Next Decade**
C. Fred Bergsten
January 2005   ISBN 0-88132-380-2

**Does Foreign Direct Investment Promote
Development?**   Theodore H. Moran,
Edward M. Graham, and Magnus Blomström,
eds.
April 2005   ISBN 0-88132-381-0

American Trade Politics, 4th ed.   I. M. Destler
June 2005   ISBN 0-88132-382-9

**Why Does Immigration Divide America?
Public Finance and Political Opposition to
Open Borders**   Gordon H. Hanson
August 2005   ISBN 0-88132-400-0

Reforming the US Corporate Tax
Gary Clyde Hufbauer and Paul L. E. Grieco
September 2005   ISBN 0-88132-384-5

The United States as a Debtor Nation
William R. Cline
September 2005   ISBN 0-88132-399-3

**NAFTA Revisited: Achievements and
Challenges**   Gary Clyde Hufbauer and
Jeffrey J. Schott, assisted by Paul L. E. Grieco and
Yee Wong
October 2005   ISBN 0-88132-334-9

**US National Security and Foreign Direct
Investment**   Edward M. Graham and
David M. Marchick
May 2006   ISBN 978-0-88132-391-7

**Accelerating the Globalization of America: The
Role for Information Technology**
Catherine L. Mann, assisted by Jacob Funk
Kirkegaard
June 2006   ISBN 978-0-88132-390-0

Delivering on Doha: Farm Trade and the Poor
Kimberly Ann Elliott
July 2006   ISBN 978-0-88132-392-4

**Case Studies in US Trade Negotiation, Vol. 1:
Making the Rules**   Charan Devereaux,
Robert Z. Lawrence, and Michael Watkins
September 2006   ISBN 978-0-88132-362-7

**Case Studies in US Trade Negotiation, Vol. 2:
Resolving Disputes**   Charan Devereaux,
Robert Z. Lawrence, and Michael Watkins
September 2006   ISBN 978-0-88132-363-2

C. Fred Bergsten and the World Economy
Michael Mussa, ed.
December 2006   ISBN 978-0-88132-397-9

Working Papers, Volume I   Peterson Institute
December 2006   ISBN 978-0-88132-388-7

WORKS IN PROGRESS

China's Energy Evolution: The Consequences of Powering Growth at Home and Abroad Daniel H. Rosen and Trevor Houser

Global Identity Theft: Economic and Policy Implications Catherine L. Mann

Globalized Venture Capital: Implications for US Entrepreneurship and Innovation Catherine L. Mann

Forging a Grand Bargain: Expanding Trade and Raising Worker Prosperity Lori G. Kletzer, J. David Richardson, and Howard F. Rosen

Why Reform a Rich Country? Germany and the Future of Capitalism Adam S. Posen

Global Forces, American Faces: US Economic Globalization at the Grass Roots J. David Richardson

The Impact of Global Services Outsourcing on American Firms and Workers J. Bradford Jensen

Policy Reform in Rich Countries John Williamson, ed.

Banking System Fragility in Emerging Economies Morris Goldstein and Philip Turner

Aligning NAFTA with Climate Change Objectives Meera Fickling and Jeffrey J. Schott

Private Rights and Public Problems: The Global Economics of Intellectual Property in the 21st Century Keith Maskus

The Positive Agenda for Climate Change and Trade Trevor Houser, Jacob Funk Kirkegaard, and Rob Bradley

Stable Prices, Unstable Currencies: The Weak Link between Exchange Rates and Inflation and What It Means for Economic Policy Joseph E. Gagnon

Carbon Abatement Costs and Climate Change Finance William R. Cline

A Decade of Debt Carmen M. Reinhart and Kenneth S. Rogoff

DISTRIBUTORS OUTSIDE THE UNITED STATES

Australia, New Zealand,
and Papua New Guinea
D. A. Information Services
648 Whitehorse Road
Mitcham, Victoria 3132, Australia
Tel: 61-3-9210-7777
Fax: 61-3-9210-7788
Email: service@dadirect.com.au
www.dadirect.com.au

India, Bangladesh, Nepal, and Sri Lanka
Viva Books Private Limited
Mr. Vinod Vasishtha
4737/23 Ansari Road
Daryaganj, New Delhi 110002
India
Tel: 91-11-4224-2200
Fax: 91-11-4224-2240
Email: viva@vivagroupindia.net
www.vivagroupindia.com

Mexico, Central America, South America,
and Puerto Rico
US PubRep, Inc.
311 Dean Drive
Rockville, MD 20851
Tel: 301-838-9276
Fax: 301-838-9278
Email: c.falk@ieee.org

Asia (*Brunei, Burma, Cambodia, China,*
Hong Kong, Indonesia, Korea, Laos, Malaysia,
Philippines, Singapore, Taiwan, Thailand,
and Vietnam)
East-West Export Books (EWEB)
University of Hawaii Press
2840 Kolowalu Street
Honolulu, Hawaii 96822-1888
Tel: 808-956-8830
Fax: 808-988-6052
Email: eweb@hawaii.edu

Canada
Renouf Bookstore
5369 Canotek Road, Unit 1
Ottawa, Ontario KlJ 9J3, Canada
Tel: 613-745-2665
Fax: 613-745-7660
www.renoufbooks.com

Japan
United Publishers Services Ltd.
1-32-5, Higashi-shinagawa
Shinagawa-ku, Tokyo 140-0002
Japan
Tel: 81-3-5479-7251
Fax: 81-3-5479-7307
Email: purchasing@ups.co.jp
For trade accounts only. Individuals will find
Institute books in leading Tokyo bookstores.

Middle East
MERIC
2 Bahgat Ali Street, El Masry Towers
Tower D, Apt. 24
Zamalek, Cairo
Egypt
Tel. 20-2-7633824
Fax: 20-2-7369355
Email: mahmoud_fouda@mericonline.com
www.mericonline.com

United Kingdom, Europe
(*including Russia and Turkey*)**, Africa,**
and Israel
The Eurospan Group
c/o Turpin Distribution
Pegasus Drive
Stratton Business Park
Biggleswade, Bedfordshire
SG18 8TQ
United Kingdom
Tel: 44 (0) 1767-604972
Fax: 44 (0) 1767-601640
Email: eurospan@turpin-distribution.com
www.eurospangroup.com/bookstore

Visit our website at:
www.piie.com
E-mail orders to:
petersonmail@presswarehouse.com